Descriptosaurus Story Writing

Descriptosaurus Story Writing provides a resource for younger pupils that will not only expand their descriptive vocabulary but also provide them with models that demonstrate 'language in action,' in a genre that is popular and familiar to children aged 5–9. Providing the essential building blocks to create a narrative text, alongside contextualised banks of vocabulary, phrases and sentence types, this book is designed to provide young pupils with the opportunity to see how a text is constructed using words, phrases and sentences. This exciting new resource:

★ Provides vocabulary for setting, character, 'show not tell' and sensory descriptions with clearly defined progression
★ Demonstrates how to use this vocabulary in different contexts using set sentence structures
★ Offers four model narratives written in different styles and levels of difficulty
★ Presents modelled sentences with exercises so that pupils can expand their vocabulary
★ Enables young pupils to develop their understanding of how sentences are constructed and become more confident about using these skills in their own story writing.

This is an ideal resource to dramatically improve children's knowledge and understanding of language, grammar and punctuation for all KS1 and KS2 primary English teachers, literacy coordinators and parents. This easily accessible guide will also be helpful for teachers to use in preparation for Spelling, Punctuation and Grammar (SPAG) alongside a creative writing task.

Alison Wilcox is a Law and Economics graduate from Cardiff University, who worked as a primary-school teacher for many years. Whilst teaching, she developed *Descriptosaurus* to scaffold and improve children's creative writing, with dramatic results, and she made the decision to give up full-time teaching to work on the *Descriptosaurus* series. To keep up to date with current practices in schools, Alison undertakes brief teaching assignments, works with schools to develop new resources and conducts workshops for schools and teaching alliances.

Adam Bushnell was a primary-school teacher and is now a published author of both fiction and academia. He has had fifteen books published for children and six books published for teachers on the teaching of writing. He works as a 'visiting author' in the UK and internationally, delivering writing workshops for primary school aged children. He also offers CPD (Continuing Professional Development) for schools and delivers keynote speeches at conferences about reading and writing in education.

Descriptosaurus Story Writing

Language in Action for Ages 5–9

Alison Wilcox
and Adam Bushnell

Routledge
Taylor & Francis Group

LONDON AND NEW YORK

First published 2021
by Routledge
2 Park Square, Milton Park, Abingdon, Oxon OX14 4RN

and by Routledge
605 Third Avenue, New York, NY 10017

Routledge is an imprint of the Taylor & Francis Group, an Informa business

© 2021 Alison Wilcox and Adam Bushnell

British Library Cataloguing-in-Publication Data
A catalogue record for this book is available from the British Library

Library of Congress Cataloging-in-Publication Data
Names: Wilcox, Alison, author. | Bushnell, Adam, author.
Title: Descriptosaurus story writing: language in action for ages 5-9 /
Alison Wilcox & Adam Bushnell.
Identifiers: LCCN 2020038750 | ISBN 9780367559113 (hardback) |
ISBN 9781003095675 (ebook)
Subjects: LCSH: Creative writing (Elementary education) |
Description (Rhetoric)–Study and teaching (Elementary) |
Vocabulary–Study and teaching (Elementary)
Classification: LCC LB1576 .W487595 2021 | DDC 372.62/3–dc23
LC record available at https://lccn.loc.gov/2020038750

ISBN 13: 978-0-367-55911-3 (hbk)
ISBN 13: 978-1-00-309567-5 (ebk)

Typeset in Myriad Pro
by Deanta Global Publishing Services, Chennai, India

Printed and bound in Great Britain by
TJ Books Limited, Padstow, Cornwall

Dedication and acknowledgement

This book was completed during the coronavirus crisis. We would, therefore, like to dedicate it to all those key workers who put themselves at risk for the greater good.

Thanks to Bruce Roberts of Routledge for his continued support, advice and unwavering confidence in the *Descriptosaurus* concept.

To all those teachers who once again made a tremendous effort to provide their pupils with online learning resources and support to ensure that their learning suffered the least disruption possible.

I would personally like to extend my particular thanks to Wayne Thomas, a truly wonderful, kind, compassionate human being, whose assistance and support was invaluable to my elderly parents and eased the anxiety about their welfare for my sister and myself. Thank you, Wayne, from the bottom of my heart.

Thanks to my daughter, Kitty, my wonderful, personal technology 'helpline'!

Alison

Thank you for the continued love, support and belief from all my family and friends.

Adam

Contents

Introduction   ix
How to use this book   xi

Part 1: Settings: Landscapes   1

1   Forests and woods   3
2   Hills and mountains   9
3   Seas and oceans   14
4   Islands and beaches   19
5   Caves   23
6   Modern street   28
7   Sounds   32
8   Smells   38
9   Touch   41
10 Sun   45
11 Wind   47
12 Rain   50
13 Thunder and lightning   53

Part 2: Characters   55

14 Characters' appearance   57
15 Characters (heroes) – personality   61
16 Characters (heroes) – animals   64
17 Characters (villains) – personality   76
18 Characters (villains) – animals   80
19 Defeating a villain   86
20 Dialogue   90

Part 3: Resources for 'Language in action'   93

21 'The Ninjabread Girl'   95
22 Modelled sentences   97
23 Innovating sentences model   100
24 Coordination and subordination   102
25 'Captain Moody and his pirate crew'   104
26 Modelled sentences   109
27 Innovating sentences model   114
28 Coordination and subordination   116
29 'Ruby Red'   119
30 Modelled sentences   123
31 Innovating sentences model   131

vii

Contents

32 Coordination and subordination   135

33 'Jack and the Crystal Fang'   144

34 Modelled sentences   152

35 Innovating sentences model   168

36 Coordination and subordination   173

Part 4: 'Language in action' templates   191

Plot outline   193

Scene outline   195

Collecting descriptive words and phrases   196

Sentence parts and structure   197

Stretching a sentence   199

Experimenting with vocabulary and sentences   200

Introduction

It is widely accepted that high levels of literacy developed at a young age will greatly enhance the educational development of a child in all subject areas, not just English. To be able to develop these skills, children need contextualised vocabulary, frameworks, models and descriptive references delivered in an easy-to-use, flexible and engaging format.

Descriptosaurus is widely used in schools, but its accessibility is limited for the younger age group. This age group would also greatly benefit from a resource that provides the opportunity to expand and use descriptive vocabulary, but also one that enables them to explore 'language in action,' by demonstrating how to use this vocabulary in different contexts using set sentence structures.

With an increasing focus on explicit teaching of vocabulary, it is evident that the methods used ensure that children learn, understand and are given the opportunity to use new vocabulary regularly. However, it is important that this focus is also done within the context of a writing task, where the pupils themselves are seeking to widen their repertoire rather than learning random new words chosen for them within the context of an artificial scenario.

Descriptosaurus treats learning to write like learning a new language, and thus the words and phrases are grouped into categories which can be accessed for a particular creative writing task. The design of this new resource for younger pupils has taken this a step further by using a table format to, for example, group nouns and adjectives in complementary categories and the relevant verbs listed in the same order. This format provides different levels of scaffolding to meet the needs of individual pupils as well as different age groups with a clear progression for writing development. For example, the tables can be copied and cut up to investigate new vocabulary and the construction of phrases. The phrases can be used to experiment with different combinations to construct sentences by physically using the strips and experimenting with alternatives.

The sentences are split into two levels, which can be used either as models appropriate to the age group or to provide pupils with an opportunity to investigate and discuss the next step in their progression.

This new younger version of *Descriptosaurus* demonstrates the use of vocabulary, grammar and punctuation for effect and constructing meaning. Providing such a resource for younger pupils gives them a sound basis and knowledge of sentence structure, grammar and punctuation that can act as a springboard for more complex vocabulary and writing conventions, which is important and is now the focus of the new Ofsted Framework with the spotlight on demonstrating pupil progress in the writing process.

As well as providing the building blocks to create a text, with contextualised banks of vocabulary, phrases and sentence types, it is also designed to provide young pupils with the opportunity to spend time with a model text, deconstructing it into words, phrases and sentence types; to look at it in a number of different ways so that pupils not only expand their

Introduction

vocabulary but also that the structures become embedded in their minds. This ensures that less of their working memory must be used as they tackle the difficult task of writing a narrative and, therefore, allows more time for their own ideas when innovating a text or inventing their own.

In the Resource Section are four model narratives. They have been written in four different styles and cover the age range of this book. However, each of the stories can be used, innovated or deconstructed according to the level, experience and knowledge of each age group, class or individual pupil. Even the youngest pupil will be able to acquire vocabulary, phrases and different sentence structures from these models.

Each of the texts is broken down into modelled sentences appropriate for KS1 and LKS2, and exercises are provided where pupils can apply the descriptive vocabulary from the main part of the book and the texts to expand their vocabulary in a set structure.

There are also exercises where sentence stems are provided and the pupils practise coordination and subordination by completing the sentence with their own idea and descriptive phrases.

By reading the stories, breaking them down, working with them in smaller chunks and innovating the structures, they not only acquire knowledge of constructing a sentence and text, but also become more confident about using what they have learned when inventing their own stories.

Descriptosaurus Story Writing is intended to complement the highly effective and popular Talk 4 Writing process by providing children with the opportunity to practise different parts of the writing process and experiment with the language and structure of a story before writing it as a whole text. It is in essence 'Writing 4 Writing,' or 'Language in Action.'

The model texts can also be used by teachers to develop their own models appropriate to the developmental levels of the pupils in their class. In KS1 and LKS2, and in fact in any one class, there can be a big difference in the knowledge, experience and literacy skills of the pupils. The aim is to provide a resource that allows pupils to progress at their own level.

Whilst we have provided four stories (two innovations on familiar tales and two new stories) with different styles and levels of difficulty, they are intended to demonstrate how any text can be used alongside *Descriptosaurus* to develop vocabulary, sentence and text structure.

This is another step on the *Descriptosaurus* journey and we are sure it is one that will help younger pupils become enthusiastic and confident writers with the necessary building blocks to ensure that they will be ready, willing and able to participate fully in the writing process as they move onto the next stage.

How to use this book

Planning a piece of writing is an essential part of the writing process. This is often the skill that young pupils find the most difficult. However, if they are taught the skills and given an easy-to-use structure from an early age, planning will become a habit that will benefit them as they develop their writing skills and tackle other aspects of the writing process.

The templates are included in the Resource Section.

STEP 1: AN OUTLINE – BASED ON THE STORY OF RED RIDING HOOD

The first step is to develop a simple outline for the story by completing the table shown below:

TEMPLATE		EXAMPLE	
Setting:		Setting:	Forest
Hero/heroine:		Hero/heroine:	Red Riding Hood (RRH)
Villain:		Villain:	Wolf
Challenge:		Challenge:	To deliver basket to granny
Problem:		Problem:	Wolf was waiting for her in Granny's cottage
Result:		Result:	Rescued by woodcutter who cut off the wolf's head

STEP 2: BREAKING THE TEXT INTO SCENES

Breaking down a text into scenes is another helpful step for teaching planning skills. This means that the text is broken down into manageable bite-size chunks. It also assists with developing a beginning, middle and end structure.

Identifying key words for setting, characters and events are also useful skills in developing writing and lead to exploring vocabulary description for each element.

TEMPLATE		EXAMPLE	
Scene:		Scene:	RRH enters the forest
Keywords:		Keywords:	RRH, Granny, forest, path, flowers, birds, squirrels, sunny

STEP 3: USING DESCRIPTOSAURUS TO COLLECT VOCABULARY

Once the keywords and events have been identified, use the word bank template shown below to expand the planning.

1. List the nouns that would be found in the setting.
2. Take each noun and expand on description, which can be an adjective or a more specific noun, for example, flowers – bluebells, snowdrops, daffodils.
3. Verbs can be added between the text boxes.

SCENE 1: **Red Riding Hood** enters the **forest**
Keywords: Ruby, Granny, forest, path, flowers, birds, squirrels, sunny

NOUNS	DESCRIPTION
Red Riding Hood	excited
forest	thick, deep
trees	tall
sky	blue, sunny
branches	crooked
leaves	bright green
path	narrow, winding
flowers	
birds, magpies	singing
squirrels	scampering

_____

_____

_____

_____

_____

SCENE 2: **Red Riding Hood** is lost in the **forest**
Keywords: Red Riding Hood, wolf, forest, path, dark, scared

NOUNS		DESCRIPTION
Ruby		scared
wolf		big, bad
forest		thick, dense
trees, branches		crooked
roots		twisted
sky		light, misty, dark
twigs, thorns		sharp, spiky
path		narrow, winding
sounds		snap, crack
animals		wolf
heart		jumped, thudded
		shout, yell, scream

_____

_____

_____

_____

_____

STEP 4: COLLECTING DESCRIPTIVE PHRASES

Use the phrases table to pick out favourite descriptive phrases to include in the text.

WORDS		PHRASES
NOUNS	**DESCRIPTION**	
Red Riding Hood, cloak, basket	Excited, skipping, humming Red, bread, cakes	Red cloak, black, curly hair, blue eyes
Forest, trees, branches, leaves, flowers	Thick, deep, tall	Tall, majestic trees Thick forest of enormous trees Huge treetops like green umbrellas
Paths	Narrow, winding	Narrow path wound …

Sky	Blue, sunny	Beautiful bright sunlight
Birds, animals	Squirrels, magpies	Scampering squirrels Flew from branch to branch
Sounds	Singing, rustling	Chattering magpies
Smells	Flowers, fruit	Juicy fruit, fresh flowers

STEP 5: SENTENCE PARTS AND STRUCTURE

This is an opportunity to practise identifying parts of speech and using the vocabulary and phrases in a simple sentence structure within the context of a creative piece of writing.

EXAMPLE 1

Step 1: **Noun**	What is your sentence about? **(branches)**
Step 2: **Adjective**	Describe it/them. **(thick, twisted)**
Step 3: **Verb**	What does it/they do? **(spread)**
Step 4: **Prep. Phrase**	Where or when? **(across the path)**
Step 5:	Create a complete sentence

The / thick, twisted / branches / spread / across the path.
    Adjective(s)   /   noun   / verb   / prepositional phrase

EXAMPLE 2

Step 1: **Noun**	flowers
Step 2: **Adjective(s)**	yellow
Step 3: **Verb**	hung
Step 4: **Prepositional phrase**	from the branches
Step 5: **Complete sentence**	Yellow flowers hung from the branches.

	Example 1	Example 2	Example 3
Noun:	branches	flowers	
Adjective:	thick, twisted	yellow	
Verb:	spread	hung	
Prepositional Phrase:	across the path	from the branches	
Sentence:	The thick, twisted branches spread across the path. Yellow flowers hung from the branches.		

STEP 6: INNOVATION

To embed the sentence structure, change each part of speech individually in a step-by-step process. This activity serves to reinforce knowledge of parts of speech and sentence structure in a written context as opposed to merely identifying the individual components in a series of de-contextualised sentences.

Exercise A

1. **Change the noun:**
   Thick, twisted **branches** spread across the path.
   Thick, twisted **roots** spread across the path.
   Thick, twisted _____ spread across the path.
2. **Change the adjective(s):**
   Thick, twisted roots spread across the path.
   Huge, crooked roots spread across the path.
   _____ roots spread across the path.
3. **Change the verb:**
   Huge, crooked roots **spread** across the path.
   Huge, crooked roots **wriggled** across the path.
   Huge, crooked roots_____ across the path.
4. **Change the prepositional phrase:**
   Huge, crooked roots wriggled **across the path**.
   Huge, crooked roots wriggled **over the ground**.
   Huge, crooked roots wriggled _____

Exercise B

1. **Change the noun:**
   Yellow **catkins** hung from the trees.
   Yellow **flowers** hung from the trees.
   Yellow _____ hung from the trees.
2. **Change the adjective(s):**
   Yellow flowers hung from the trees.
   Long, crimson flowers hung from the trees.
   _____ flowers hung from the trees.
3. **Change the verb:**
   Long, crimson flowers **hung** from the trees.
   Long, crimson flowers **dangled** from the trees.
   Long, crimson flowers _____ from the trees.
4. **Change the prepositional phrase:**
   Long, crimson flowers dangled **from the trees**.
   Long, crimson flowers dangled **from the branches**.
   Long, crimson flowers dangled _____.

STEP 7: JOINING SENTENCES

1. Coordination

Investigation using sentence stems

Investigation is the key to developing knowledge and confidence in joining sentences. This can be done in the following ways:

(a) Use the main clause strips in Part 3 and investigate by placing each of the coordinating clauses in turn with the sentence stem and deciding which makes sense.
(b) The table below contains sentence stems and two alternative coordinating main clauses, (a) and (b). One of them clearly connects to the sentence stem. Pupils tick the correct main clause to complete the compound sentence.

Clause (1)	Conjunction	Clause (2)	√
It was a sunny day	and	a. the forest was covered in misty light.	
		b. the forest was covered in bright sunlight.	
Red Riding Hood was excited	and	a. skipped along the path.	
		b. crept along the path.	
Her mother warned Red Riding Hood not to wander off the path	but	a. she soon kept her promise.	
		b. she soon forgot her promise.	
The forest was full of the sound of birds singing	and	a. the rustle of leaves.	
		b. loud music.	
Red Riding Hood was sure she was being followed	and	a. she kept looking behind her.	
		b. she started singing.	
She heard the magpies chattering	but	a. she could not see them.	
		b. she stopped to watch.	
A twig snapped behind her	and	a. Red Riding Hood fell on her knees.	
		b. Red Riding Hood froze.	
Her heart thudded in her chest	but	a. she kept on walking.	
		b. she hid behind the bush.	

Red Riding Hood began to shout	but	a. she was scared.	
		b. no-one heard her.	
Red Riding Hood turned around	and	a. closed her eyes.	
		b. her eyes were wide with shock.	

2. Subordination

Main Clause	Conjunction	Subordinate Clause	√
Red Riding Hood really wanted to pick bluebells for Granny	because	a. they made her sneeze.	
		b. they were her favourite flowers.	
Her mum had warned Red Riding Hood to stay on the path	because	a. it was a sunny day.	
		b. wolves and gnomes lived in the forest.	
She kept stumbling	because	a. it was too dark to see the roots across the path.	
		b. she fell over.	

STEP 8: JOINING SENTENCES (THE NEXT LEVEL):

Cut the two tables into strips. Take one table at a time and mix the main clauses. Pupils join the main clauses to form compound and complex sentences.

TABLE 1
SENTENCE STEMS AND CONJUNCTIONS
It was a sunny day **and**
The narrow path twisted through the forest **and**
Clusters of pink and white blossoms hung from the branches **and**
She spotted lots of dazzling bluebells **and**
Her mother had warned Red Riding Hood not to wander off the path, **but**
She was determined to pick some bluebells for Granny **because**
The forest was full of the sound of birds singing **and**
Magpies chattered from every tree **and**
Red Riding Hood watched the squirrels scampering up the trees **and**
Red Riding Hood set off back towards the main path, **but**

MAIN CLAUSES
they were her favourite flowers.
flew from branch to branch to hide their stolen treasures.
was covered in petals like pink confetti.
she couldn't find her way back.
the path was covered in beautiful bright sunlight.
sitting on a branch to nibble their nuts.
the rustle of leaves as they flew from tree to tree.
she decided to pick some for her grandmother.
she soon forgot her promise.
vivid, lime green vines wound around the huge tree trunks.

TABLE 2
SENTENCE STEMS AND CONJUNCTIONS
She walked deeper and deeper into the forest **and**
Red Riding Hood kept stumbling over the tangle of twisted roots that wriggled across the path **because**
She was sure she was being followed **and**
Patches of misty light shone through the trees **and**
This part of the forest was very quiet, **so**
Red Riding Hood started to walk faster and faster, **but**
Red Riding Hood's heart was thudding in her chest **and**
Behind her, she heard the snap of a twig **and**
Red Riding Hood spun around **and**
MAIN CLAUSES
it was difficult to see them in the gloom.
every small sound made Red Riding Hood jump.
she began to shout louder and louder.

the tangle of bushes and thorns grabbed at her coat and trousers.
made the crooked trees look like ghostly figures.
her eyes widened with horror.
she kept looking over her shoulder.
the trees were now knotted together to form an arch over her head.
she kept stopping to look over her shoulder.

Innovate

Complete the sentence stems with own main clauses.

Exercise 1: Combining the phrases into sentences and into a paragraph

Using *and, but, because* and *so* to develop sentence structure.

Complete the following sentence stems:
1. It was a sunny day **and** _____.
2. The narrow path twisted through the forest **and**_____.
3. Clusters of pink and white blossoms hung from the branches **and**_____.
4. Red Riding Hood spotted lots of bluebells, which were like a dazzling carpet of jewels **and**_____.
5. Her mother had warned Red Riding Hood not to wander off the path, **but**_____.
6. She was determined to pick some bluebells for Granny **because**_____.
7. The forest was full of the sound of birds singing **and**_____.
8. Magpies chattered from every tree **and**_____.
9. Red Riding Hood watched the squirrels scampering up the trees **and**_____.
10. Once she had collected a large bunch of bluebells, Red Riding Hood set off back towards the main path, **but**_____.
11. She had walked deeper and deeper into the forest **and**_____.
12. Red Riding Hood kept stumbling **because**_____.
13. She was sure she was being followed **and**_____.
14. Patches of misty light shone through the trees **and**_____.
15. This part of the forest was very quiet, **so**_____.
16. Red Riding Hood started to walk faster and faster, **but**_____.
17. Her heart was thudding in her chest, **but**_____.
18. Behind her, Red Riding Hood heard the snap of a twig **and**_____.
19. Red Riding Hood spun around **and**_____.
20. Beside her, there was a_____.

STEP 9: STRETCHING THE SENTENCE

To add more detail to a sentence, practise 'stretching' it by asking the following questions:

STRETCHING A SENTENCE	
Who?	
Is doing What?	
When?	
Where?	
Why?	

STRETCHING A SENTENCE: Example	
Who?	Red Riding Hood
Is doing What?	turned back
When?	after she had picked lots of bluebells for Granny
Where?	towards the main path
Why?	because it was getting dark

STEP 10: DRAMA: DEVELOPING UNDERSTANDING OF 'SHOW NOT TELL' AND USEFUL PHRASES

1. Act out the scene. What will you do with your hands? How will you stand? What will happen to your mouth and eyes? How will you move?
2. Make a list of phrases that describe the actor's actions and facial expressions.

STEP 11: REVISION: ADDING DETAIL TO IMPROVE THE DESCRIPTION

Brainstorming ideas to improve description:

1. What can Red Riding Hood see when she enters the forest?
2. What are the flowers like? What can she hear? What can she smell?
3. Describe the forest. Describe the weather.
4. How does Red Riding Hood feel?
5. Describe the forest as Red Riding Hood moves away from the path deeper into the forest.
6. What can she see? What can she hear?
7. Describe the moment she realises she is being followed by the wolf. How does she feel?
8. What does the wolf look like?

STEP 12: MODELS: IDENTIFYING DESCRIPTION USING SIGHT, SOUND AND SMELL

Read the paragraph above and highlight phrases that:

★ Help to paint a vivid picture of the scene – sights, sounds, smells, touch.
★ Describe how Red Riding Hood was feeling.
★ Use a simile.
★ Contain noun phrases.
★ Contain actions or other verbs.
★ Reveal Red Riding Hood's character.

SCENE 1: SENTENCES 1–10

It was a sunny day and the path was covered in beautiful bright sunlight. The narrow path twisted through the forest and was covered in petals like pink confetti. Clusters of pink and white blossoms hung from the branches, and vivid, lime green vines wound around the huge tree trunks. Red Riding Hood spotted lots of bluebells, which were like a dazzling carpet of jewels, and she decided to pick some for her grandmother. Her mother had warned Red Riding Hood not to wander off the path, but she soon forgot her promise. She was determined to pick some bluebells for Granny because they were her favourite flowers. The forest was full of the sound of birds singing and the rustle of leaves as they flew from tree to tree. Magpies chattered from every tree and flitted from branch to branch to hide their stolen treasures. Red Riding Hood kept stopping to watch the squirrels scampering up the trees and then sitting on a branch to nibble the nuts clutched between their tiny fingers. Finally, she set off back towards the main path, but she couldn't find her way back. She was lost!

SCENE 2: SENTENCES 11–20

Red Riding Hood walked deeper and deeper into the forest and the trees here formed a dark arch over her head. She kept stumbling because a tangle of twisted roots wriggled across the path and it was difficult to see them in the gloom. She was sure she was being followed and she kept stopping to look over her shoulder. Patches of misty light shone through the trees and made the crooked trees look like ghostly figures. This part of the forest was very quiet, so every small sound made Red Riding Hood jump. She started to walk faster and faster, but the tangle of bushes and thorns grabbed at her coat and trousers. Red Riding Hood's heart was thudding in her chest and she kept looking over her shoulder. She heard the snap of a twig and froze. Then, she began to shout louder and louder, but no one heard her. All of a sudden, Red Riding Hood spun around, and her eyes widened with horror. Beside her, there was a wolf.

Part 1
Settings:
Landscapes

1
Forests and woods

NOUNS	ADJECTIVES
Forest, jungle, woods **Trees**, bushes	**Thick**, bushy, deep, dense **Beautiful**, lovely, amazing, stunning, majestic **Tall**, high, towering **Huge**, enormous, gigantic, massive
Leaves, bark, twigs, flowers, petals, fruit, berries, nuts **Bluebells**, snowdrops, daffodils, poppies **Ivy**, nettles, thorns, moss **Trunk**, branches, roots, logs	**Brown**, yellow, gold, bronze **Green**, olive, mint, lime, emerald **Red**, scarlet, crimson **Bright**, colourful, vivid, dazzling **Rough**, sharp, spiky, scratchy, prickly, thorny **Bent**, twisted, crooked **Dead**, rotting
Floor, paths, trails **Sun**, sunlight **Wind**, breeze **Rain**, dew, frost, ice **Mist**, fog **Darkness**, shadows	**Wide**, narrow **Straight**, winding, twisting **Light**, sunny, bright **Shining**, sparkling, twinkling, glittering **Gentle**, fierce **Dark**, black, gloomy **Wet**, damp, cold, chilly, icy **Misty**, foggy **Scary**, creepy, spooky, ghostly
Smell, scent, perfume **Stink**, stench	**Sweet**, fresh, minty, fruity, nutty **Stale**, sour, musty, damp, rotten, mouldy, disgusting, revolting

1 Settings: forests and woods

Sound, noise **Hum**, whisper, click, rustle **Tweet**, chirp, cheep, hoot, chatter **Snap**, creak, groan, crash, thud **Cry**, howl, shriek, screech	**Quiet**, soft, gentle, pleasant, bright, cheerful **Loud**, echoing **Snapping**, creaking, groaning, crashing, thudding, pounding **Howling**, shrieking, screeching

VERBS
Stood, rose, climbed **Spread**, stretched, arched, bent
Covered, wrapped, blanketed, cloaked
Wound, crept, wriggled
Stopped, blocked, trapped
Knotted, twisted, tangled
Grabbed, grasped, gripped, pulled, tugged
Scratched, tore
Hung, dangled, drooped
Swayed, floated, fluttered, danced, hopped
Shone, lit, sparkled, shimmered
Heard, drifted, filled, echoed
Smelt, wafted

PHRASES (Nouns and adjectives)	PHRASES (Verbs)
deep, dark wood	spread out in front of me
thick wood of enormous trees	stretched as far as the eye could see
tall, majestic trees (*like a crowd of green umbrellas*)	rose above my head
huge treetops (*like an emerald blanket*)	blocked out the sky
beautiful, mint green vines	dangled from the branches
gigantic, olive green leaves	drooped from the branches
dazzling, lime green stems	wound around the branches
vivid, lime green vines	twisted around the huge tree trunks
leaves (*like emerald green ribbons*)	fluttered in the breeze
narrow path	twisted through the forest

path through the forest	was covered in beautiful bright sunlight
carpet of bluebells (*like a path of dazzling jewels*)	covered the forest floor
colourful ivy (*like party streamers*)	hung between the trees
chattering magpies	flitted from branch to branch
	hid their stolen treasures
scampering squirrels	sat on a branch
	nibbled the nuts
	clutched the nuts between their tiny fingers
groups of snowdrops	nodded in the breeze
crisp, fiery red autumn leaves	hopped and danced across the floor
red and orange berries	covered the bushes
clusters of bright blossoms	drooped from the branches
amazing colourful petals	covered the path
leaves (*like green feathers*)	danced in the wind
groups of lovely yellow blossoms	hung between the branches
colourful juicy fruit	dangled from the branches
carpet of pink petals	covered the forest floor
bright red poppies	swayed in the wind
sparkling frost	covered the branches
beautiful bright sunlight	lit up the path
massive, crooked trees	blocked the path
thick, twisted branches and tangled undergrowth	made it impossible to find a way through
enormous roots	spread across the path
rotting leaves and dead branches	hid the path
tangle of twisted roots	tripped me up
enormous tangled roots	wriggled across the path
sharp thorns	scratched my arms and legs
twigs (*like black, spiky spider legs*)	grabbed at my coat
rough, peeling bark	tore my trousers

pointed leaves (*like fingernails*)	grasped at my arms
twisting trail	was cloaked in a blanket of darkness
patches of misty light	shone through the trees
blanket of fog	crept over the forest
crooked trees (*like ghostly statues*)	could be seen through the mist
fluttering leaves	rustled in the breeze
hum of insects	drifted through the wood
bending branches	creaked in the wind
towering trees	creaked and groaned as they swayed
snap of a twig	made me jump
sound of scrabbling claws	tearing at the trunk
screech of a hunting owl	tore through the woods
scent of fresh flowers	drifted through the wood
stink of damp, rotting leaves	filled the air

SENTENCES

Level 1	Level 2
The forest was a beautiful place.	The forest was a beautiful place, but hidden somewhere inside was a secret, ancient wood.
The ancient forest was creepy.	The secret, ancient forest loomed ahead of me.
The ancient forest was very dark and deep.	The dark, dense wood spread as far as the eye could see.
I could not see the other end of the forest.	The forest was thick and tangled and it was impossible to see a way through.
The trees were huge.	The tall, majestic trees towered above me.
The huge trees hid the sky.	Above my head, the gigantic trees were *like a crowd of green umbrellas* shielding the sky.
The huge trees had bright green leaves.	The huge trees were covered in a cloak of vivid green leaves.
The sun sparkled on the bright green leaves.	The sun danced on the emerald green leaves.
The forest was full of colourful flowers.	The forest was ablaze with brightly coloured flowers.

There were snowdrops and bluebells.	Groups of snowdrops, bluebells and daffodils nodded in the breeze.
	A white blanket of snowdrops danced in the frosty air.
There were lots of bright yellow daffodils on the ground and long catkins on the branches.	The bright yellow daffodils swayed in the wind.
	Long, hairy catkins dangled from the branches.
There were gigantic pink toadstools.	The forest floor was buried in gigantic toadstools like vivid pink and yellow umbrellas.
She walked on a carpet of pink petals.	A carpet of pink petals covered the forest floor.
There were rotting leaves on the path.	A blanket of damp, rotting leaves hid the path.
There were lots of colourful fruit and berries on the trees and bushes.	Colourful juicy fruit dangled from the branches.
	Plump, brightly coloured berries covered the bushes.
She could smell the plump, juicy berries.	The sweet, enticing scent of ripe berries drifted through the air.
There was frost on the branches.	Frost sparkled on the branches.
She could not find the secret path.	The tangled branches leaned over the path and hid the trail.
She was lost in the dark wood.	It was impossible to find a way through the dark, twisting, tangled wood.
The path was blocked by huge trees.	The thick, tangled trees twisted together to block the path.
The path was blocked by enormous branches and roots.	Enormous roots wriggled across the path.
	Dead branches *like huge bleached limbs* littered the path.
Thorns scratched my legs.	Needle-sharp thorns scratched at my arms and legs.
Twigs caught on my coat.	Twigs *like spiky spider legs* grabbed at my coat.
Sharp leaves tugged at my hair.	Pointed leaves *like fingernails* twisted my hair.
The forest was misty.	The forest was cloaked in mist.
	The forest was covered in a veil of mist.
	Misty light shone through the trees.
	A creepy green fog filled the wood.
I walked as quickly as I could.	I walked faster and faster.

My heart raced.	My heart thudded in my chest.
I looked behind me.	I kept glancing over my shoulder.
My eyes were wide.	My eyes widened with horror.
I stopped.	I froze.
I called for help.	I shouted louder and louder.
	I screamed at the top of my voice.

2
Hills and mountains

NOUNS	ADJECTIVES
Hill, mountain, cliff **Top**, peak, summit	**Tall**, high, towering **Huge**, enormous, gigantic, massive **Beautiful**, amazing, magical, enchanting, mystical **White**, snowy, snow-capped, icy, frozen **Dark**, grey, black, gloomy **Rocky**, sharp, pointed, jagged, craggy
Slope, climb, drop **Path**, track, trail **Ledge**, ridge	**Hard**, difficult, dangerous, deadly **Steep**, vertical **Narrow**, winding, twisting **Flat**, level
Ground **Rock-face**, rocks, boulders, stones, pebbles, gravel	**Smooth**, slippery **Rough**, uneven, bumpy
Snow, ice **Icicles**, stalagmites, stalactites	**Frosty**, icy, frozen, freezing **Sharp**, needle-like, spiky
Streams, rivers, waterfalls	**Clear**, crystal, silver, sparkling, glittering, glinting **Bubbling**, trickling, babbling, tumbling **Wild**, frothing, roaring, thundering
Wind, breeze, gusts, gale **Clouds**, mist, fog	**Cold**, chilly, icy **Dark**, thick, dense, freezing

VERBS
Surrounded, circled
Rose, climbed, stretched, towered, soared, ascended
Fell, dropped, dived, plunged, descended
Climbed, wound, twisted, snaked
Spread, crept, slithered, drifted, wrapped
Covered, coated, blanketed, shrouded
Hid, concealed, camouflaged
Dotted, scattered
Blocked, obstructed, trapped
Hung, dangled
Rose, shot up, sprouted, burst, erupted
Shone, sparkled, shimmered, glittered, glinted
Flowed, trickled, tumbled, slid, bubbled, danced, poured, rushed, gushed, hurtled
Splashed, gurgled, babbled, roared, thundered
Blew, gusted, whistled, whined, howled, screeched, shrieked

PHRASES (Nouns and adjectives)	PHRASES (Verbs)
massive mountains	surrounded me
dark, dangerous mountain	rose in front of me
huge, snowy mountains	climbed towards the sky
enormous, snow-capped peaks	filled the sky
high hills (*like giant's shoulders*)	towered above the village
gigantic mountains (*like the humps of a dinosaur*)	stretched as far as my eye could see
	soared towards the land of the gods
enormous mountain peak	touched the clouds
towering summits	soared above me
black, deadly peaks	rose in front of me
pointed, icy peak (*like a dagger*)	cut through the clouds

jagged peaks	were covered in ice
magical world of snow and ice	shimmered in the bright sunlight
steep cliff	dropped vertically beneath me
steep, slippery, rock-face	glinted with ice
steep, deadly cliffs	protected the ancient town from attack
narrow, rocky path	wound up the side of the mountain
	twisted and turned
	snaked towards the summit
huge black boulders	blocked the path
	were dotted across the track
thick fog	hid the top of the mountain
blanket of fog	covered the valley
veil of mist	crept over the rocks
	wrapped around the hills (*like ghostly arms*)
freezing fog	hid the summit
blanket of black clouds	covered the peaks
bubbling streams	trickled down the hill
	flowed downhill from the top of the mountain
rivers (*like silver ribbons*)	tumbled down the slopes
	slid down the side of the cliff like a snake
	splashed over the rocks
enormous waterfalls wild, frothing waterfalls	poured out of the cliff
	rushed down the mountain
	roared down the rock-face
glittering ice	covered the peak
ice (*like glass*)	sparkled from the summit
huge pointed icicles (*like spears*)	hung from the ledge
stalagmites (*as sharp as swords*)	rose from the ground
enormous pillars of ice	erupted out of the ground

SENTENCES	
Level 1	**Level 2**
I was surrounded by huge, snowy mountains.	I had arrived at a magical world of snow and ice.
Huge mountains filled the sky.	Massive, snow-capped mountains stretched as far as the eye could see.
	Gigantic, snowy mountains, *like the humps of a dinosaur*, soared towards the land of the gods.
The icy peaks touched the sky.	The jagged, icy peaks tore a hole in the clouds.
The snowy peak sparkled in the sunlight.	The snow-capped peak shimmered in the bright sunlight.
I had to climb the steep slope to the top.	I had to climb the sheer deadly slope to the summit.
There was a narrow path up the mountain.	I spotted a narrow path winding up the side of the mountain.
Huge boulders blocked the path.	Huge boulders had rolled down the mountain and blocked the path.
The mountain was covered in thick fog.	Thick, freezing fog wrapped around the mountain.
Dark clouds filled the sky.	A blanket of black clouds hid the summit.
Streams trickled down the hills.	Bubbling streams tumbled down the slopes.
A river tumbled down the mountain.	A river, like a silver ribbon, snaked down the side of the mountain.
A waterfall poured down the mountain.	A wild, frothing waterfall roared down the rock-face.
The peak was covered in ice.	Glittering ice shimmered on the peak.
There were huge pillars of ice outside the cave.	Huge pointed icicles *like spears* hung above the ledge outside the cave.
The mountain was covered in mist.	Freezing fog wrapped around the slopes like ghostly arms.
Mist crept over the rocks.	A blanket of mist drifted over the peaks and slid over the slope.
The wind whistled round my head.	The whistling wind pulled and pushed at me.
I heard a hawk screech.	A hawk screeched from the ridge.
I cut my fingers on the sharp rocks.	The jagged rocks scratched my hands.

The cold wind blew in my face.	The icy wind froze my cheeks and blistered my lips.
I climbed over the boulders.	I jumped from boulder to boulder.
I pulled myself up the rock.	I grabbed the rock and tried to haul myself up on to the ledge.
I started to climb.	I took a deep breath and started to climb.
I was too tired to climb to the top.	My arms and legs were aching.
	I did not think I was going to make it to the top because I was too tired to go any further.

3
Seas and oceans

NOUNS	ADJECTIVES
Sea, ocean	**Blue**, lapis, green, emerald, silver, white, clear, crystal **Sparkling**, glittering, shimmering
Surface, depths	**Grey**, black, dark, inky, murky **Calm**, flat, smooth **Rough**, choppy **Deep**, shallow
Waves **Surf**, foam, spray, mist	**Small**, little **Soft**, gentle **Huge**, giant, vast, enormous, massive **Wild**, fierce, brutal **Loud**, roaring, deafening
Island, shore, beach, bay, rock-pool **Sand** **Rocks**, pebbles, stones	**Sandy**, rocky **White**, golden, sugary, powdery **Rough**, soft, smooth **Shiny**, polished
Shells, seashells	**Round**, oval **Star-shaped**, horn-shaped, petal-shaped, conical
Seaweed	**Wet**, slimy, squishy **Black**, brown, green, red
Seagulls, crabs, jellyfish	
Sky	**Blue**, grey, black, dark, cloudy, stormy
Sun, sunlight, rays	**Bright**, sunny, dazzling

Breeze, wind	**Warm**, gentle **Cold**, icy, chilly, strong, fierce
Clouds, rainclouds	**White**, grey, dark, black **Fluffy**, wispy, thick, dense

VERBS
Spread, stretched, surrounded
Shone, sparkled, glowed, glittered, shimmered
Rippled, creased, wrinkled
Foamed, swirled, churned
Rolled, slid, crept, trickled
Grew, rose, curved, arched
Rushed, raced, marched, galloped
Fell, tumbled, dropped
Hit, struck, bashed, crashed, smashed
Slapped, swished, sloshed, splashed
Hissed, whooshed, groaned, growled, roared, boomed
Rocked, swayed, tossed
Wrapped, clung, pulled, tugged, dragged
Screeched, shrieked
Dived, swooped

PHRASES (Nouns and Adjectives)	**PHRASES (Verbs)**
sparkling blue sea	surrounded the island
sea around the island	was a shimmering blue
huge blue ocean	stretched as far as the eye could see
giant lapis blue ocean	rolled below a clear sky
bright blue water of the ocean	sparkled with sunlight
emerald surface	was as calm as a pond
crystal clear water	rippled with sunlight

silky surface of the sea	rippled beneath a cloudless sky
	glittered in the golden sun
streaks of light	shimmered across the surface of the water
choppy grey sea	tossed the boat from side to side
dark, icy water	churned under the stormy sky
dark, murky depths	swirled beneath the boat
inky black depths of the ocean	waited for me beneath the boat
black rocks (*like giant teeth*)	rose from the surface
soft white foam	slid onto the sand
	rolled gently onto the beach
	trickled into the rock-pools
crystal waves	wrinkled the surface
small waves	curled around the rocks
emerald seaweed	floated on the surface
slimy, green seaweed	wrapped around my legs
polished shells like petals	shone beneath the surface
smooth cone-shaped shells	clung to the rocks
	formed a line at the edge of the water
huge black wave	rose from the sea
	grew bigger and bigger
giant black wave	rose in an arch
	curved towards the beach
	roared towards the boat
wave after wave	smashed onto the rocks
	crashed against the rocks
	pounded the shore
hissing foam	covered the rocks in an icy mist
soothing swish, splash, slosh of the waves	trickling onto the beach
boiling foam	smashed into the side of the surfboard
battered boat	sank beneath the surface

smell of salt-water and seaweed	floated through the air
warm breeze	carried the smell of salt-water
huge white seagull	swooped down towards me
	screeched above my head

SENTENCES

Level 1	Level 2
The sea was bright blue.	The sparkling bright blue sea surrounded the island.
The huge blue sea stretched in front of me.	The huge blue ocean stretched as far as I could see.
The sea sparkled with sunlight.	The emerald surface rippled with sunlight below a clear blue sky.
The water was crystal clear and as smooth as silk.	The silky, crystal clear surface of the water rippled in the breeze.
	Streaks of light shimmered across the surface of the clear water.
The boat went up and down in the rough, grey sea.	The choppy, grey sea tossed the boat from side to side.
The dark, icy water swirled around my legs.	The dark, icy water churned and swirled around my legs and tried to drag me under.
The water under the boat was murky and deep.	Beneath the surface, the dark murky depths of the sea stretched down and down.
I could not see anything through the dark, murky water.	The inky black depths of the ocean waited for me beneath the boat.
I was surrounded by huge, black rocks.	Black rocks *like giant teeth* rose from the surface around me.
Soft white foam slid onto the sand.	The edge of the wave was fringed with soft, white foam.
Small waves rolled gently onto the sand.	Small waves trickled onto the sand and curled around my feet.
Slimy seaweed wrapped around my legs.	Huge strands of slimy green seaweed wrapped around my legs.
Beautiful shells like petals sparkled in the sand.	Beautiful, cone-shaped shells clung to the rocks.
	Polished shells like horns formed a line at the edge of the water.

A black wave rose from the sea.	A giant black wave swelled in the sea and grew bigger and bigger.
The huge black wave curved towards the boat.	The giant black wave rose in an arch and roared towards the boat.
It smashed onto the rocks.	It crashed against the rocks and covered me in an icy mist.
The waves crashed over my head.	The boiling foam smashed into the side of my surfboard and crashed onto my head.
The boat sank beneath the wave.	The battered boat rolled onto its side and slowly sank beneath the surface.
The waves swished and splashed onto the beach.	I listened to the soothing swish, splash, slosh of the waves.
I could smell salt-water.	The smell of salt-water and seaweed floated through the air towards me.
	The warm breeze carried the smell of salt-water.
A huge seagull screeched above my head.	A huge white seagull screeched as it swooped down towards my head.

4
Islands and beaches

NOUNS	ADJECTIVES
Sea, ocean, reef, waves, surf	**Shallow**, deep **Blue**, green, emerald
Coral **Fish**, clownfish, pufferfish, lionfish **Sharks**, dolphins, fin	**Red**, violet, purple, black **Beautiful**, colourful, stunning, amazing **White**, maroon, yellow, orange, rainbow-coloured, striped, spotted **Spiky**, spiny **Grey**, sleek
Island	**Flat**, rocky **Tropical**, desert **Small**, large, long, thin, narrow, wide **Wild**, overgrown, black, empty, deserted
Cliffs, caves	**Steep**, sheer **Tall**, high
Forest, wood, trees, palm trees, coconuts	**Large**, thick, dense
Beach, shore, sand, dunes **Rocks**, pebbles, shingle	**Golden**, white, sandy, powdery, pebbly, rocky
Bones, skeletons, wrecks, wood, timber, driftwood	**Old**, ancient, white **Crooked**, knobbly, cracked, rotten, battered, splintered

Chest, treasure, relics **Cups**, plates, jugs, coins **Jewels**, necklaces, bracelets, rings, sapphires, rubies, emeralds, diamonds	**Wooden**, metal **Gold**, silver **Sparkling**, glittering

VERBS
Found, situated, located
Surrounded, circled
Hid, sheltered, guarded, protected
Stood, lined, stretched
Sloped, dropped, descended
Trapped, ship-wrecked, marooned
Covered, dotted, scattered, littered, layered
Swayed, rocked, rolled, flapped, quivered, fluttered
Swum, glided, darted **Jumped**, dived
Hidden, buried, scattered, piled, heaped
Shone, sparkled, shimmered, glittered, glowed

PHRASES (Nouns and Adjectives)	PHRASES (Verbs)
small tropical island	surrounded by emerald green water
	circled by a shallow reef
wide, sandy island	shadowed by a deep, tropical jungle
narrow, rocky island	surrounded by the deep ocean
desert island	was wild and overgrown
	was lined with enormous palm trees
huge, jagged rocks	guarded the entrance to the island
stunning coral reef	lay beneath the surface of the water
coral, *like black pillars*,	rose from the seabed
purple coral, *like a fan*,	flapped below the rocks
feathery, red coral	swayed on the rocks
crusted spines, *like furry fingers*,	waved in the current

coral, *like brightly painted bushes,*	sprouted from the rocks
beautiful, multi-coloured coral reef	was dotted with tropical fish
rainbow-coloured fish	darted through the water
spiked puffer fish	swam around the coral
red, white and maroon striped lionfish	flashed between the coral
orange and white striped clownfish	circled the rocks
curved grey tips of shark fins	sliced through the water behind the reef
sand dunes, *like a mountain range,*	hid the secret cove
flat, sandy cove	was sheltered by high, steep cliffs
black mouths of numerous caves	were carved into the cliffs
steep smooth cliffs	rose vertically up out of the sea
rocky cliffs	towered above the sea
golden sandy beach	stretched for miles
powdery white sand	shimmered in the blazing sun
huge leaves, *like a fan,*	curved from the top of the palm tree
large umbrella palm trees	provided shelter from the blazing sun
groups of coconuts	dangled from the palm trees
white human and animal bones	were scattered over the beach
skeletons, skulls and jawbones	littered the beach
gaping jaw of an enormous mammal	blocked the mouth of the cave
huge, crooked pieces of driftwood	were scattered over the sand
objects from ancient shipwrecks	were dotted across the beach
relics from ancient times	were scattered over the bay
battered remains of a ship	torn to pieces on the rocks
	washed ashore during the storm
huge wooden treasure chest	carved with strange symbols
	buried in the sand under the palm tree
golden plates, cups and jugs	were piled high at the back of the cave
piles of jewels – sapphires, rubies, diamonds and emeralds	glittered from the bottom of the box
fistfuls of gold coins	glinted in the sand
	trickled onto the sand

SENTENCES	
Level 1	**Level 2**
It was a small, sandy island.	In front of me was a small, sandy island.
I could see a narrow, rocky island in the middle of the ocean.	A narrow, rocky island rose from the middle of the ocean.
It was surrounded by emerald green water.	The small, tropical island was surrounded by emerald green water.
There was a coral reef around the island.	A beautiful coral reef circled the island.
There was a colourful coral reef below the surface.	A stunning, rainbow-coloured coral reef lay beneath the surface of the water.
Purple coral swayed on the rocks.	Purple coral, *like a fan*, swayed on the rocks.
Orange stripy fish swam around the reef.	Rainbow-coloured fish darted through the water.
I could see a shark's fin in the water.	The grey tip of a shark's fin sliced through the water.
The island was empty.	The island was deserted.
Huge rocks blocked the entrance to the island.	Huge, jagged rocks guarded the entrance to the island.
High cliffs rose out of the sea.	High, rocky cliffs rose vertically out of the sea.
There was a long, sandy beach.	The golden, sandy beach stretched for miles.
Huge leaves curved from the top of the palm tree.	Huge leaves, *like a fan,* curved from the top of the palm tree.
Coconuts hung from the tall trees.	Coconuts dangled from the huge umbrella palm trees.
Bones were scattered over the sand.	Bleached white human and animal bones were scattered over the beach.
Objects from old shipwrecks were dotted across the beach.	Objects from an ancient shipwreck were scattered around the battered remains of the ship.
I found a huge treasure chest buried in the sand.	According to the map, the treasure chest was buried in the sand under the palm tree.
The chest was full of gold plates, coins and jewels.	Piles of jewels, sapphires, rubies and diamonds glittered from the bottom of the box.
Gold coins sparkled in the sun.	Fistfuls of gold coins trickled onto the sand.

5
Caves

NOUNS	ADJECTIVES
Hill, mountain, cliff, rock, rock-face **Cave**, opening, mouth, entrance	**Secret**, ancient **Amazing**, wonderful, spectacular **Small**, big, huge, giant, enormous
Roof, ceiling	**Low**, high, deep
Walls, floor, path	**Smooth**, wet, damp, slippery **Rough**, sharp, jagged **Sandy**, rocky, stony
Tunnels, passage, maze	**Winding**, twisting, turning
Bats, spiders, snakes, rats	**Swooping**, slithering, scuttling, scratching, scrabbling
Water, stream, pool, lake **Icicles**, stalagmites, stalactites	**Blue**, green, clear **White**, glassy, crystal **Bright**, shining, sparkling, glittering, shimmering
Carvings, pictures, signs, symbols, code **Paint**, chalk, clay, charcoal **Horses**, deer, stags, bull, bison, boar, lions, bear, wolf **Eagle**, hawk **Dragons**, phoenix, unicorns, centaur	**Old**, ancient, prehistoric, ice-age, stone-age **Red**, yellow, brown, black **Colourful**, realistic, life-like, detailed **Strange**, mysterious, magical
Fossils, relics, artefacts **Bones**, skeleton, skull, teeth	**Rough**, cracked, smooth, polished
Weapons, tools, arrowheads, tips, blades, pottery	**Wood**, stone, flint, clay, bronze, iron

5 *Settings: caves*

Sound, voice, hiss, whisper, shriek, laughter, echo **Scratch**, scuttle, drum, beat, thud, boom	**Soft**, loud, echoing **Scary**, ghostly
Light, rays, torch, beam **Darkness**, shadows	**Bright**, dim **Dark**, black, inky, gloomy, shadowy
Smell, stench, reek	**Wet**, damp, mouldy, sickly, stale, musty

VERBS
Opened **Led**, stretched, spread **Bent**, twisted, turned, wound, split, divided
Rose, grew, covered **Hung**, dangled
Sparkled, glittered, shimmered, glistened
Dripped, bubbled, trickled, poured, gushed
Chalked, painted **Carved**, chiselled, engraved, etched
Found, discovered, dug, excavated
Heard, listened to, made out **Whispered**, murmured, hissed, cackled **Beat**, drummed, scratched, scuttled, thudded, boomed, echoed
Shone, lit, reflected **Saw**, revealed
Smelt, sniffed **Drifted**, wafted
Scared, shocked, spooked **Excited**, eager, thrilled

PHRASES (Nouns and Adjectives)	PHRASES (Verbs)
narrow gap in the rock	led to a low, small cave
behind the thick, tangled vines	was the mouth of an enormous cave
opening to the cave	was a black hole in the rock-face
hole the size of a small door	led to an enormous cave

maze of low, dark tunnels	led off from the entrance
narrow passage	branched off to the right
narrow, winding path	twisted and turned
	was a dark tunnel between the walls of rock
	twisted and turned as it wound deep underground
huge stalactites *like giant spikes*	hung from the ceiling
enormous stalagmites *like crystal spears*	rose from the floor
pool of bright blue water	glowed from the bottom of the pit
clouds of steam	rose from the bottom of the pit
walls at the entrance to the cave	were painted with swirling red and blue symbols
strange mathematical signs and symbols	were carved in the rock
mysterious letters from an ancient language	were chalked in white on one of the walls
colourful picture of a hunting scene	covered the entire wall
horses and deer, lions, bears and wolves	painted in red, yellow and brown on the ceiling
huge, life-like eagle	spread its wings across one corner
amazing discovery	made her eager to explore the caves
bones, fossils and artefacts	had been discovered in the cave
bronze weapons and iron tools	covered in layers of dried mud and sand
pieces of clay pottery	lay scattered over the floor of the cave
wood carvings	
flint arrowheads and blades	were frozen in the ice
	were preserved in the ice
narrow beam from the torch	was the only light
small crack in the ceiling	was the only source of light
flickering light	made shadows dance on the walls
strip of light from a crack in the ceiling	lit up the floor of the cave
inky blackness	surrounded her
rush of cold air	brushed her face

5 Settings: caves

flurry of furry wings	beat the air above her head
hundreds of bats	flapped above her head
colony of bats	swooped from the ceiling
drip, drip of water	made a ghostly sound in the silence of the cave
sound of ghostly whispers	drifted towards her
deafening boom	echoed through the cave

SENTENCES

Level 1	Level 2
A gap in the rock led to a small cave.	The entrance to the small cave was a narrow gap in the rock.
Thick vines hid the entrance to the cave.	Behind the thick, tangled vines was the mouth of an enormous cave.
The opening to the cave was a big black hole in the cliff.	The entrance to the cave was a big hole like a black mouth in the cliff-face.
It was a huge cave with lots of tunnels.	A maze of low, dark tunnels led off from the huge cave.
A narrow winding path twisted down underground.	A narrow path twisted and turned between the walls of rock as it wound deep underground.
Huge stalactites hung from the ceiling.	Huge stalactites *like giant spikes* descended from the ceiling.
Enormous stalagmites rose from the floor.	Enormous stalagmites *like crystal spears* rose from the floor.
There was a pool of bright blue water at the bottom of the pit.	Clouds of steam rose from a pool of glowing, bright blue water at the bottom of the pit.
Red and blue symbols were painted on the walls.	The walls at the entrance to the cave were painted with swirling red and blue symbols.
Strange signs were carved in the rock.	Strange mathematical signs and symbols had been carved in the rock.
The wall was covered by a picture of a hunt.	A colourful, detailed picture of a boar hunt covered the entire wall.
Stone-age tools and weapons had been found in the cave.	The amazing discovery of stone-age tools and weapons made her eager to explore the caves.
Pieces of pottery were buried under the earth.	Pieces of clay pottery were covered in layers of dried mud and sand.

She found flint blades and arrowheads in the ice.	Flint arrowheads and blades had been frozen in the ice.
The only light was from her torch.	The narrow beam from her torch was the only source of light.
Shadows moved on the walls.	A flickering light made shadows dance on the walls.
It was black.	Inky blackness surrounded her.
Bats dived down from the roof of the cave.	A colony of bats swooped down from the ceiling.
The only sound was the drip, drip of water.	The drip, drip of water made a ghostly sound in the silence of the cave.
A loud boom echoed through the cave.	A deafening boom echoed through the cave.

6
Modern street

NOUNS	ADJECTIVES
City, town, village **Landmarks** **River**, bridge	**Busy**, noisy, crowded, lively, full **Quiet**, empty, deserted **Famous**, historic
	Big, large, huge, vast, enormous, massive **Small**, little, tiny
Buildings, houses, flats, tower blocks, skyscrapers	**Tall**, high, towering
	New, modern **Old**, ancient
	Glass, metal, stone, brick, wooden
Offices, shops, hotels, markets, restaurants, cafes, doctors, dentists, hairdressers, supermarket	**Grand,** beautiful, majestic **Shiny**, bright, clean, polished
	Dirty, grimy, rotting, crumbling, run-down, rickety
School, college, university	**Colourful**, red, yellow, orange, green, grey, golden
	Black, dark, grey, polluted
Museum, art gallery, library, cinema, theatre **Church**, mosque, temple, synagogue **Dome**, tower, minaret, spire, steeple	**Domed**, arched

Park, parkland, playground	**Wide**, narrow
Slides, swings, sports pitches	**Long**, short
Fences, railings, gates, entrances	**Straight**, circular, winding, twisting, crooked
Road, street, pavement, alley, path **Traffic**, cars, vans, trucks, buses **Pedestrians**, pedestrian crossing, traffic lights, **Car park**	**Smooth**, rough, cobbled, bumpy, potholed
Rubbish, litter, plastic bags, plastic bottles, packets, papers **Graffiti** **Smoke**, fumes, pollution	

VERBS
Found, located, situated
Live, play, work, visit, tour
Stand, perch, line, arch
Scatter, spill **Cover**, spread, stretch, sprawl
Built, made of, constructed
Look, overlook, tower, loom **Can be seen**
Buzz, bustle, hurry, rush, stream **Fill**, crowd **Wait**, queue
Shine, glint, sparkle **Darken**, shadow
Spray, paint
Heaped, piled
Belch, pollute

PHRASES (Nouns and Adjectives)	PHRASES (Verbs)
busy, colourful city	buzzing with activity
large, busy town	filled with traffic and people
small village	hidden at the foot of the mountain

tiny village	overlooks the sea
tall glass skyscrapers	soar skyward
huge tower blocks	huddle together
long wide, straight street	lined with shops
scores of shops, galleries and museums	scattered all over the city
huge children's play area	full of swings and slides
big green areas of parkland	filled with sports pitches and playgrounds
tables and chairs from cafes and restaurants	spill out onto the streets
elaborate entrance to the Grand Hotel	stands out from the other buildings
quaint tearooms	spread out along the river
long, stone bridge	arches over the river
polished glass windows	look out onto the busy street
line of people	wait at the traffic lights
red brick school building	is set back off the road
two lines of rectangular glass windows	glint from behind the high metal railings
beautiful stained-glass windows of the ancient church	sparkle in the bright sun
golden dome-shaped roof of the temple	can be seen from across the city
tall minaret of the mosque	can be seen above the rooftops
streams of noisy traffic	belch their grey fumes into the air
piles of rotten rubbish	heaped at the side of the pavement
plastic bottles and packets	scattered over the road
a veil of smoke	hangs over the town
bright red, yellow and orange graffiti	covers the walls under the bridge
metal shutters	block the windows
broken glass	litters the pavement
wooden boards	cover the windows of the old library

SENTENCES	
Level 1	**Level 2**
It is a busy, colourful city.	The busy, colourful city is buzzing with activity.
It is a large, busy town.	The large, busy town is filled with traffic and people.
There is a small village at the bottom of the mountain.	The small village is hidden at the foot of the mountain.
The tiny village is by the sea.	The tiny village is perched on the cliffs overlooking the sea.
There are tall glass skyscrapers.	The tall glass skyscrapers soar skyward.
There are lots of shops on the long straight street.	The long, wide, straight street is lined with shops.
The town has a big park.	In the centre of the town is a big park filled with sports pitches and playgrounds.
The hotel has a magnificent entrance.	The spectacular, elaborate entrance to the Grand Hotel stands out from the other buildings.
There is a stone bridge over the river.	A long, stone bridge arches over the river.
The school is a red brick building.	The red brick school building is set back off the road.
There are two lines of rectangular glass windows on the front of the school.	Two lines of rectangular glass windows glint from behind the high metal railings.
The church has beautiful stained-glass windows.	The beautiful stained-glass windows of the ancient church sparkle in the bright sun.
The temple has a golden dome-shaped roof.	The golden dome-shaped roof of the temple can be seen from across the city.
The mosque has a tall minaret.	The tall minaret of the mosque can be seen above the rooftops.
There are piles of rotten rubbish all over the pavement.	Piles of rotten rubbish are heaped at the side of the pavement.
There are plastic bottles, wooden cartons and packets everywhere.	Plastic bottles, wooden cartons and packets are scattered over the road.
The walls are covered in graffiti.	Bright red, yellow and orange graffiti covers the walls under the bridge.
The windows are covered by wooden boards.	Wooden boards cover the windows of the old library.

7
Sounds

NOUNS	ADJECTIVES
Sound, noise, echo, silence **Humans**, people **Voices**, tone, calls, shouts, cries, yells, screams **Giggles**, snorts, laughter **Whispers**, murmurs, sighs, moans **Animals**, creatures, dogs, cats, horses, rats, mice, bats, snakes **Hiss,** grunt, growl, whine, bark, yelp, howl, roar **Purr**, coo, neigh, whinny **Squeal**, shriek	**Loud**, noisy, deafening, ear-splitting
	Soft, quiet, faint, gentle, weak
	Dull, dim, hushed, muffled, stifled
	High, squeaky, shrill, high-pitched
	Low, husky, croaky, rasping
	Bright, cheerful, joyful, beautiful, melodious
	Happy, excited, enthusiastic
	Horrible, nasty, cold, evil, sneering
Movement, feet, footsteps, boots, heels, hooves, paws, claws, wings **Floorboards**, clock, pipes, door, lock, hinges, window **Creak**, rattle, bang, tick, chime, ring **Traffic**, car, tyres, horn, engine **Stones**, rocks, pebbles **Trees**, branches, twigs, leaves	**Scary**, frightening, terrifying, threatening, blood-curdling, spine-chilling
	Odd, strange, unusual, mysterious, secretive
	Ghostly, eerie, sinister
	Clumsy, awkward, lumbering, shuffling
	Sad, miserable, gloomy, mournful
	Humming, honking, screeching, roaring
	Creaking, clicking, groaning, rattling, banging
	Slithering, skittering, scuttling, padding, thudding, pounding

Water, stream, river, waterfall, sea, waves **Wind**, breeze, gust, gale **Rain**, hail, storm, thunder	**Trickling**, bubbling, gurgling, splashing, crashing
	Whispering, murmuring, whining, howling, roaring
	Hissing, streaming, pelting, beating **Rumbling**

VERBS
Heard, made out, listened for
Sounded, drifted, filled, surrounded **Rang**, echoed
Said, spoke, called
Sang, hummed, whistled
Giggled, snorted, laughed
Whispered, sighed, murmured, mumbled
Whined, gasped, moaned, groaned, squealed
Shouted, yelled, cried, wailed, screamed, screeched, shrieked
Growled, grunted, barked, yelped, howled
Purred, cooed, neighed, whinnied
Hissed, buzzed, warbled, chirruped, trilled, hooted
Bawled, bleated, croaked
Moved, crept, slithered, shuffled, scuttled
Ran, sprinted, thudded, pounded
Scratched, clawed, scraped
Fluttered, flapped, whirred
Clicked, ticked, chimed, creaked, clinked, rattled, rustled, crackled, crunched, cracked, snapped, banged, blared
Bubbled, trickled, gurgled, lapped, swished, splashed, crashed
Rumbled, boomed, thundered
Beat, drummed, rang, throbbed

PHRASES (Nouns and Adjectives)	PHRASES (Verbs)
soft, murmuring sounds	filled the cave
sudden, loud noise	made her jump
deafening sound	echoed through the building
soft, misty voice	whispered through the door
high-pitched laughter	came from the cupboard
faint wheezing	came from behind the door
croaky voice	crackled on the line
piercing screech	echoed along the passage
panicked voices	came from the next room
piercing, spine-chilling scream	ripped through the silence
eerie, mournful cry	sprang from the shadows
blood-curdling scream	came from down the passage
scratching sound	began in the corner of the room
scrape of sharp claws	came from the other side of the door
whine of a mosquito	kept him awake
shrill click of crickets	rose from the bushes
eerie mournful cry	came from high in the trees
screech of an owl	
blood-curdling shriek	came from the attic
joyful birdsong	woke her at dawn
trill of blackbirds	rose from the trees
sound of chattering magpies	drifted through her bedroom window
ancient hinges	creaked in the breeze
rusty key	groaned as it turned in the lock
wooden floorboards	creaked as the footsteps shuffled closer
creaks and rustles of the old house	kept her awake
huge, shuffling feet	moved closer and closer to her hiding place
squeak of a boot heel	woke her up
thud of pursuer's feet	moved closer and closer

smash of broken glass	made her heart race
sickening crash	made her hold her breath
whine of traffic	could be heard in the distance
honk of a car horn	startled her
gunshot of a car backfiring	made her jump
screech of tyres	came from the next street
snap of a twig	shattered the silence
dry leaves	crunched under her feet
sound of dripping water	echoed through the cave
gentle sound of lapping water	sent her to sleep
deafening roar of a waterfall	pounded in his ears
rumble of a huge wave	soaring towards the shore
a gentle breeze	whispered through the trees
a breath of wind	
howling gale	rattled the windows
sheets of rain	drummed on the roof
ghostly silence	wrapped around the house
deathly quiet	thudded in their ears
her gasping breath	was the only sound in the room
throbbing silence	made her feel uneasy
silence as thick as fog	made her tense
silence like a thick blanket	made her pulse race

PREPOSITIONAL PHRASES	PREPOSITIONAL PHRASES
out of the shadows	in the passage ahead of him
outside the door	from far off in the building
somewhere at the back of the room	from somewhere inside
outside the window	from up the stairs
behind the window	from behind the wall
behind the curtain	around the house
close to his shoulder	through the wall

35

near his ear	along the passage
through the air	under her feet
all around them	above her head

SENTENCES

Level 1	Level 2
She heard soft murmuring sounds.	She heard soft murmuring sounds coming from the back of the cave.
A sudden, loud noise made her jump.	A sudden, loud noise just behind her made her jump.
She heard a soft, misty voice.	A soft, misty voice whispered through the door.
She heard high-pitched laughter.	High-pitched laughter came from the direction of the cupboard.
There was a croaky voice on the phone.	A croaky voice crackled down the phone.
There was a blood-curdling scream.	A blood-curdling scream came from down the passage.
She could hear the scrape of claws on the wooden door.	Sharp claws scraped on the wooden door.
The sound of the mosquito kept her awake.	The whine of a mosquito kept her awake.
There was a horrible shriek.	A blood-curdling shriek came from down the passage.
The sound of joyful birdsong woke her up.	She was woken at dawn by joyful birdsong.
She could hear the chattering of magpies.	The sound of a chattering magpies drifted through her bedroom window.
The door creaked.	The rusty key groaned as it turned in the lock.
Footsteps moved closer to her hiding place.	Huge footsteps shuffled closer and closer to her hiding place.
The sound of breaking glass scared her.	The smash of breaking glass made her heart race.
She could hear traffic outside.	The whine of traffic could be heard in the distance.
A car horn made her jump.	The honk of a car horn made her heart race.
A twig snapped.	The snap of a twig shattered the silence.

She could hear dripping water.	The sound of dripping water echoed through the cave.
There was a gentle breeze.	A gentle breeze whispered through the trees.
The gale howled.	The howling gale rattled the windows.
It was quiet.	The ghostly silence wrapped around the house.
It was deathly quiet.	The deathly silence thudded in her ears.
The only sound was her own breathing.	Her gasping breath was the only sound in the room.

8
Smells

NOUNS	ADJECTIVES
Air, breeze, draught, waft, whiff	**Nice**, lovely, pleasant, refreshing, comforting
Smell, scent, perfume, odour, aroma **Fruity**, apple, banana, citrus, orange, lemon, lime, rhubarb **Lavender**, honeysuckle, mint, roses, lilies, pine needles, grass **Cocoa**, chocolate **Soap**, washing powder, toothpaste, polish, disinfectant, bleach	**Clean**, fresh, sweet **Perfumed**, fragrant, aromatic **Minty**, fruity, flowery, nutty **Mild**, faint, strong, powerful, pungent **Hot**, spicy, tangy
Stink, stench, reek, odour **Damp**, dust, mould **Fumes**, petrol, smoke, pollution **Seaweed**, salt **Socks**, trainers **Sweat**, perspiration **Eggs**, milk, meat, fish, cheese **Onions**, garlic	**Nasty**, sickly, horrible, unpleasant **Dirty**, stinking, foul, rank, revolting **Stale**, stuffy, dusty, musty **Damp**, mouldy **Sour**, sharp, bitter, acidic, salty **Rotten**, decaying **Sweaty**, cheesy, fishy, garlicky
Nose, nostrils, breath, throat	

VERBS
Smelt, smelt of, scented **Breathed in**, inhaled
Crept, drifted, floated, wafted, blew, seeped, spread
Filled, burst, rushed **Left**, stayed, remained, hung, lingered

Covered, cupped
Tickled, stung, choked, coughed, vomited
Made her/him think of …   **Reminded** her/him of …   **Brought back** memories of …

PHRASES (Nouns and Adjectives)	PHRASES (Verbs)
whiff of fresh minty toothpaste	wafted towards him
sweet scent of lavender spray	filled the bathroom
pleasant smell of pine needles	made him think of Christmas
refreshing lemon scent	floated through the air
clean smell of washing powder	came from his shirt
whiff of honeysuckle	blew through the open window
air in the room	smelt fresh and sweet
tangy scent of lemon juice	tickled his nostrils
whiff of melted chocolate	seeped from the microwave
delicious smell of roast chicken	made her hungry
scent of spicy curry	filled the kitchen
comforting smell of apple pie	reminded him of his grandmother
dirty sports socks	gave off a smell of rot and sweat
foul smell of cheesy trainers	rose from his bag
	seeped under the wardrobe door
sickly stench of rotten eggs	filled the fridge
horrible reek of rotting meat	made him feel sick
sour smell of stale milk	burst from the bottle
powerful whiff of chopped onions	made her eyes water
nasty stink like rotting flesh	forced him to cover his mouth
	made him hold his breath
powerful, sickly stench of petrol fumes	stung his nostrils
	made him cough
stale smell of dust and damp	hung in the air

foul stink of mouldy cheese	lingered in the kitchen
revolting stench of stale sweat	made him retch
	made his stomach churn

SENTENCES

Level 1	Level 2
He could smell fresh minty toothpaste.	A whiff of fresh minty toothpaste wafted towards him.
There was a sweet smell of lavender in the bathroom.	The sweet scent of lavender filled the bathroom.
She could smell washing powder.	The clean smell of washing powder came from his shirt.
There was a smell of honeysuckle.	A whiff of honeysuckle blew through the open window.
He breathed in the smell of lemon juice.	When he inhaled, the citrus scent of lemon juice tickled his nostrils.
There was a delicious smell of roast chicken.	The delicious smell of roast chicken made her stomach rumble.
He could smell apple pie.	The comforting smell of apple pie reminded him of his grandmother.
The dirty sports socks stank.	The dirty sports socks gave off a smell of rot and sweat.
The trainers smelt foul.	A foul smell of cheesy trainers seeped under the wardrobe door.
The smell of rotten eggs made him feel sick.	The sickly stench of rotten eggs made his stomach churn.
The smell of petrol made him cough.	The powerful sickly stench of petrol fumes forced him to cover his mouth and hold his breath.
There was a foul smell of mouldy cheese in the fridge.	The rancid stink of mouldy cheese filled the fridge.

9
Touch

NOUNS	ADJECTIVES
Touch, feel, texture	**Round**, square, circular, rectangular, triangular
Shape, surface, edges, points	**Hollow**, solid
Material, wood, bricks, stones, pebbles, metal, plastic, rubber, leather, glass, clay	**Wooden**, metallic, rubbery **Woolly**, fluffy, furry, fuzzy
Fabric, cotton, wool, silk, satin, nylon, fur	**Hard**, rigid **Smooth**, polished, sleek
Marble, diamond, granite, slate	
Rock, pebbles, sand, earth, mud	**Soft** **Dry**, stale, crusty, crispy **Dusty**, powdery, chalky, flaky **Sandy**, gritty, grainy
Trees, bark, branch, twigs, moss, lichen, ivy, nettles **Petals**, stems, leaves	**Rough**, coarse, uneven, bumpy, lumpy, knobbly, gnarled **Spongy**, springy, squishy, flexible **Wet**, damp, soggy, mushy, squelchy **Sharp**, spiky, pointed, prickly, jagged, thorny, needle-sharp, claw-like, bristly, thistly, barbed
Birds, mammals, insects, fish **Bats**, owls, spiders, rats, mice **Wings**, feathers, fur, scales, paws, claws, talons	**Hairy**, furry, silky, woolly, shaggy **Slimy**, slippery, oily, greasy, waxy, gooey **Wrinkled**, shrivelled, withered
Temperature, warmth, heat, cold **Breath**, air, wind, breeze, draught, gust	**Warm**, hot, baking, burning, fiery, boiling, searing, scorching, scalding, blazing, blistering, sizzling **Cold**, cool, chilly, icy, freezing, glacial, raw, frosty, arctic, savage

Body, back, spine, bones **Arms**, hands, fist, fingers **Legs**, feet, ankles, shoes **Head**, neck, face, cheeks, ears, nose, nostrils, mouth, lips **Hair**, skin, nerves	

VERBS
Felt, held, touched, handled, examined
Stroked, brushed, tickled, caressed
Poked, pressed, squeezed, squished
Pushed, pulled, tugged, grabbed, clung, gripped, clutched, grasped
Moved, nudged, hit, slapped, beat, whipped, bashed, kicked
Rippled, flickered, fluttered, swished, slithered
Tore, scratched, pricked, stung, tangled
Rushed, surged, wrapped, covered, enveloped
Bent, ducked, lowered

PHRASES (Nouns and Adjectives)	PHRASES (Verbs)
hard, wooden ball	stung his fingers
glass vase	felt smooth in her hands
polished marble floor	was cold under her bare feet
squishy lump of clay	was moulded into a round bowl
rough, gritty rocks	scratched her hands
smooth, wet pebbles	slid under her feet
damp squelchy mud	sucked at her boots
knobbly bark	was peeling away from the trunk
spongy moss	brushed against her fingers
clumps of nettles	stung her ankles
his skin	was slimy like a dead fish
warm breeze	tickled his ear
	flickered over his face

needle-sharp thorns	tugged at her sleeve
jagged edges of the stones	pressed into her feet
puff of cold air	brushed against his face
icy breeze	stung her cheeks
bitter icy cold	froze her breath
blazing heat	blistered her lips
fabric as soft as velvet	stroked her arms
swish of furry wings	brushed against her face
squelchy mud	oozed over her shoes
needle-sharp twigs	tangled in her hair
jagged edges of the rusty blade	sliced open her palm
slimy water weeds	clung to her feet
cold night air	froze her cheeks
swirls of hard, icy hail	whipped her arms
scorching heat	burnt her nostrils

SENTENCES

Level 1	Level 2
The hard, wooden ball stung his hands.	The hard, wooden ball stung his hands when he tried to catch it.
The marble floor was cold.	The polished marble floor was cold and slippery under her bare feet.
She moulded the squishy lump of clay into a round bowl.	She pressed and squeezed the squishy clay until she had moulded it into a round bowl.
The rocks were rough and gritty.	The rough, gritty rocks scratched her hands.
The mud was damp and squelchy.	The damp squelchy mud sucked at her boots.
The spongy moss felt furry.	The spongy moss felt furry as it brushed against her fingers.
The warm breeze tickled her ear.	The warm breeze tickled her ear *like a feather*.
The points of the thorns were sharp.	The needle-sharp points of the thorns tugged at her sleeve.
The icy breeze blew against her cheeks.	The icy breeze stung her cheeks.
The cold wind was icy.	The bitter, icy wind froze her breath.

Furry wings brushed her face.	The swish of furry wings brushed against her face.
The mud squelched under her shoes.	The squelchy mud oozed over her shoes.
The leaves had sharp points.	The needle-sharp points of the leaves tangled in her hair.
The rusty blade had jagged edges.	The jagged edges of the rusty blade sliced open her palm.
The hail stung her arms.	Swirls of hard, icy hail whipped her arms.
It was boiling hot.	The scorching heat burnt her nostrils.

10
Sun

NOUNS	ADJECTIVES
Sky **Rainbow**	**Clear**, blue, sunny **Wonderful**, glorious
Clouds	**Wispy**
Sun **Rays**, beams	**Golden** **Bright**, brilliant, dazzling **Hazy**, shimmering
Warmth	**Warm**, balmy
Heat	**Hot**, stifling, fierce, baking, burning, scorching **Dry** **Wet**, steamy, humid

VERBS
Burst, blazed, poured, flooded, drenched
Painted, gleamed, glittered, shimmered, sparkled, dazzled
Shone, lit, glowed
Danced, flickered
Baked, burnt, scorched

10 *Settings: sun*

PHRASES (Nouns and Adjectives)	PHRASES (Verbs)
glorious arching rainbow	celebrated the end of the storm
wispy, white clouds	drifted across the vivid blue sky
beams of brilliant sunlight	blazed from a clear, blue sky
bright golden rays	glittered on the water
glittering rays of the sunlight	shimmered in a haze over the field
	poured in through the windows
	bathed the room in light
waves of heat	shimmered on the trees
	danced on the water
dazzling sun	blinded me
merciless sun	had scorched the ground
	made the ground so hot it was like walking on hot ashes
fierce sun	beat down on my head
hot humid air	covered me in a layer of sweat

SENTENCES	
Level 1	**Level 2**
There was a beautiful rainbow across the sky.	A glorious arching rainbow celebrated the end of the storm.
The sky was bright blue and there were only a few small clouds.	Wispy, white clouds drifted across the vivid blue sky.
The sunlight was very bright and the sky a clear blue.	Beams of brilliant sunlight blazed from a clear blue sky.
The sun glittered on the water.	The sun's bright golden rays glittered on the water.
The heat shimmered on the trees.	Waves of heat shimmered in a haze on the trees.
The sun blinded me.	The dazzling sun blinded me.
The ground was too hot to walk on.	The merciless sun had scorched the ground and made it so hot it was like walking on hot ashes.
The sun beat down on my head.	The fierce sun hammered on my head and stole the moisture from my mouth.
I was hot and sweaty.	The hot, humid air covered me in a layer of sweat.

11
Wind

NOUNS	ADJECTIVES
Wind **Breeze**, draught, gust **Gale**, storm **Hurricane**	**Gentle**, soft, pleasant **Cool**, fresh, refreshing **Warm**, hot, balmy **Icy**, cold, freezing, bitter **Stiff**, brisk **Wild**, violent, fierce, ferocious
Body, head, hair, eyes **Clothes** **Forest**, trees, branches, leaves	**Stinging**, tangling **Bending**, arching, swaying **Snapping**, cracking, rustling
Whisper, rustle, hiss **Whine**, moan **Howl**, screech	**Raging**, roaring **Whining**, moaning, howling, screeching
Street, road, pavement, drain **House**, roof, door, window, windowsill, shutters, gutters **Garden**, fence, shed, bins, plant pots	**Smashing**, crashing, thudding, hammering

VERBS
Tickled, brushed, stroked
Blew, wafted
Gusted, rushed, blasted, stormed
Beat, crashed, smashed, pounded, hammered
Flapped, fluttered, flew
Shook, shuddered, shivered
Tugged, pulled, pushed, flung, whipped
Swayed, rocked, bent, arched
Rustled, creaked, rattled, snapped, slammed
Whispered, rustled, whined, moaned, groaned
Roared, screamed, howled, shrieked, screeched

PHRASES (Nouns and Adjectives)	PHRASES (Verbs)
gentle breeze	was cool and refreshing
soft warm breeze	was very pleasant
gentle breeze	tickled my face
quiet whisper of the wind across the water	was a welcome relief from the hot sun
stiff breeze	rustled the leaves
brisk chilly draught	blew through a gap in the window
whining wind	whipped against my clothes
	tugged and tangled my hair
fierce wind	whined around the tent
violent gale	rattled the tiles on the roof
	sent the shed door crashing against the fence
force of the gale	sent the bins and plant pots flying across the garden
raging storm	crashed against the windows
	screamed like a boiling kettle
ferocious gale	blew open the shutter
	slammed the shutter shut
bitterly cold wind	pulled and pushed at me from all directions
	made me gasp for breath
screeching gale	bent the trees
	hammered on the window
	pounded on the door

SENTENCES	
Level 1	**Level 2**
There was a cool, gentle breeze.	The gentle breeze was cool and refreshing.
The wind whispered across the sea.	The quiet whisper of the wind across the water was a welcome relief from the hot sun.
A cold breeze blew through the window.	A brisk, chilly draught blew through a gap in the window.
The wind whined.	The whining wind whipped around my clothes and tugged and tangled my hair.
A strong wind blew around the house.	The violent gale rattled the tiles on the roof and sent the shed door crashing against the fence.
The wind was extremely powerful.	The force of the gale sent the bins and plant pots flying across the garden.
A storm was raging outside the house.	The raging storm screamed around the house like a boiling kettle and crashed against the windows.
The shutter kept banging open.	The bitter wind blew open the shutter, sent it crashing against the wall and then slammed it shut again.
The wind was so fierce I could not get my breath.	The ferocious gale made me gasp for breath as it pulled and pushed at me from all directions.
The wind blew against the windows and doors.	The screeching gale hammered on the window and pounded on the door.

12
Rain

NOUNS	ADJECTIVES
Sky, clouds, rain	**Cloudy**, gloomy, murky **Dark**, grey, black
Drizzle, shower **Downpour**	**Light**, showery **Heavy**, constant, persistent **Torrential**, relentless
Drops, raindrops, spots, stream, puddle	**Cold**, icy, chilly, freezing **Trickling**, pattering, spitting **Dancing**, jumping, exploding
Street, road, pavement, drain **House**, roof, door, window, windowsill, shutters, gutters	**Smashing**, crashing, thudding, hammering
Forest, ground, trees, branches, leaves	
Clothes, skin **Head**, neck, face, eyes, hair, arms	**Wet**, damp, soaked, sodden, sopping **Drenched**, dripping

VERBS
Blew, moved, raced
Hid, covered, blotted
Fell, drizzled, dropped, tipped, poured, streamed
Beat, drummed, pelted, crashed, lashed, hammered, pounded
Hissed, spat, spattered, splattered
Covered, flooded
Wet, soaked

PHRASES (Nouns and Adjectives)	PHRASES (Verbs)
black clouds	raced towards the mountain
huge dark storm clouds	blotted out the sun
funnel cloud like a swirling black cone	twisted down the hill
heavy drizzle	hadn't stopped most of the day
massive downpours	flooded the garden
enormous raindrops like bullets	crashed against the door
raindrops like pellets	drummed on the surface of the puddles
icy rain	stung my face and arms
	soaked me to the skin
heavy rain	lashed against the windows
	exploded on the windowsill
	hammered on the roof
	bent the trees
	drilled into my face and eyes
	blasted me like a fire hose
	pounded on my head

SENTENCES	
Level 1	**Level 2**
There were black clouds above the mountain.	Black clouds raced towards the mountain.
The sky was covered in huge dark clouds.	The huge, dark storm clouds blotted out the sun.
The cloud was like a swirling black cone.	A funnel cloud like a swirling black cone twisted down the mountain.
It had been raining all day.	The heavy drizzle hadn't stopped all day.
The garden was flooded.	The constant massive downpours had flooded the garden.
The raindrops were like bullets.	Enormous raindrops like bullets crashed against the door.
The raindrops bounced like pellets on the puddles.	Raindrops like pellets drummed on the surface of the puddles.
I was soaking wet.	The icy rain stung my face and arms and soaked me to the skin.
The rain beat down on the windows.	The heavy rain lashed against the windows and exploded on the windowsill.
The rain stung my eyes.	It was like being blasted by a fire hose as the heavy rain pounded on my head and drilled into my face and eyes.

13
Thunder and lightning

NOUNS	ADJECTIVES
Thunder **Rumble**, growl, crash, boom	**Short**, brief, sudden **Distant** **Nearby**, overhead **Low**, rumbling **Huge**, massive, mighty **Loud**, deafening **Ominous**, menacing
Lightning, flashes, light **Bolt**, blade, fork, arrow, spear **Sky**, building, roof, ground	**Quick**, rapid **Forked**, jagged **Bright**, blinding, dazzling **Flickering** **Dangerous**, scary, terrifying

VERBS
Rumbled, crashed, boomed, growled, howled, echoed
Lit, flooded, blinded, dazzled
Shot, tore, sped, streaked, flickered

PHRASES (Nouns and Adjectives)	PHRASES (Verbs)
low faint thunder	rumbled in the distance
ominous thunder	rumbled closer and closer
mighty rumble of thunder	boomed overhead
loud, menacing thunder	crashed and howled around the house
bright, jagged lightning bolts	sped across the sky
dazzling arrows of lightning	streaked across the sky
flickering forks of blinding light	flooded the sky
	lit up the sky
blinding lightning spear	streaked across the sky like a firework

SENTENCES	
Level 1	**Level 2**
I heard thunder rumbling in the distance.	Low, faint thunder rumbled in the distance.
The thunder came closer and closer.	The ominous thunder rumbled closer and closer.
There was a huge rumble of thunder nearby.	A mighty rumble of thunder boomed overhead.
A lightning bolt raced across the sky.	A bright, jagged lightning bolt sped across the sky.
The arrows of lightning were dazzling.	Dazzling arrows of lightning streaked across the sky.
The bright lightning lit up the sky.	The flickering forks of blinding light lit up the sky.
Lightning lit up the sky like a firework.	A blinding spear of lightning streaked across the sky like a firework.

Part 2
Characters

14
Characters' appearance

NOUNS	ADJECTIVES
Height	**Short**, small, little, tiny **Average**, medium **Tall**, big, large, huge, enormous
Weight **Shape** **Body**, back, chest, shoulders, legs	**Heavy**, massive, gigantic **Strong**, muscly, burly **Light**, thin, skinny, bony **Weak**, delicate
Stance, posture	**Bent**, stopped, hunched, crooked **Straight**, upright
Head, face	**Oval**, round, plump, heart-shaped, pointy **Pale**, rosy, sunburned, glowing
Eyes	**Blue**, grey, green, brown, hazel **Small**, narrow **Large**, wide, round
Mouth	**Small**, narrow, thin **Large**, wide, thick
Teeth	**Toothless**, gap-toothed **White**, sparkling **Brown**, yellow, stained **Blackened** **Straight**, crooked, chipped, pointed
Hair **Length**	**Long**, short, shaved

Colour	Red, ginger, brown, black, blonde
Style	Straight, curly, spiky, wavy, plaited, braided
Condition	Dry, frizzy, bushy Greasy Neat, tidy Wild, messy, tousled
Hands, knuckles, fingers	Smooth, soft Rough, dry, shaky, wrinkled
Nails, fingernails	Long, pointy, sharp, claw-like Dirty

VERBS
Stood, waited, towered, blocked
Moved, walked, strode, strutted   Skipped, hopped, danced, jigged   Ran, dashed, sprinted   Crept, sneaked, pattered, tiptoed   Strolled, tramped   Limped, shuffled
Scrubbed, shone, glowed   Fell, crumpled, sagged
Looked, watched, followed, stared   Saw, noticed, noted, observed   Blinked, winked, darted, flickered   Opened, widened, closed, narrowed, drooped
Rose, curved   Smiled, grinned   Pursed, pinched, puckered
Cut, combed, brushed   Tangled   Hung, flowed   Tied, held, fastened   Spiked, gelled
Lifted, moved   Held, gripped, grasped, squeezed, clenched   Waved, motioned, gestured, beckoned   Shook, trembled, tapped

PHRASES (Nouns and Adjectives)	PHRASES (Verbs)
short, thin man	stood in front of them
short man, with stumpy little legs	shuffled towards them
tiny girl	was as delicate as a china doll
small man	was as broad as a bull
girl of average height	had been spotted at the site
tall teenager	was as scrawny as a plucked chicken
enormous giant of a man	blocked the door
massive, broad-shouldered man	towered over him
huge potbelly	hung over his trousers
tall, skinny boy	had arms and legs like sticks
old man	was as crooked as a walking stick
tall woman	stood as straight as a soldier
narrow, pointed face	was deathly pale
round rosy face	scrubbed clean until it glowed
plump hamster cheeks	wobbled when he laughed
small blue eyes	twinkled with laughter
brown eyes	were filled with tears
wide green eyes	sparkled mischievously
straight white teeth	shone when he opened his mouth
brown crooked teeth	jutted out like fangs
her red hair	hung down in two long pigtails
his thick black hair	was short and spiked like a hedgehog
his tangled blonde hair	stuck up in all directions
two enormous shovel-like hands	lifted him into the air
his bony hand	felt as cold as a skeleton
her dirty, claw-like nails	tapped on the table

SENTENCES

Level 1	Level 2
He was a short, thin man.	The short, thin man stood in front of them.
He was a short man with stumpy little legs.	A short man, with stumpy little legs, shuffled towards them.
The tiny girl was very delicate.	The tiny girl was as delicate as a china doll.
They had seen a girl of average height.	A girl of average height had been spotted at the site.
The teenager was very tall and thin.	The teenager was very tall and as scrawny as a plucked chicken.
He was a massive, muscly man.	A massive, muscly man towered above her.
The old woman was crooked.	The old woman was as crooked as a walking stick.
She had a narrow, pointed face.	Her narrow, pointed face was deathly pale.
He had plump cheeks like a hamster.	His plump hamster cheeks wobbled when he laughed.
She had small blue eyes.	Her small blue eyes twinkled with laughter.
He had sad brown eyes.	His brown eyes were filled with sadness.
She had round green eyes.	Her round green eyes sparkled mischievously.
He had straight white teeth.	His straight white teeth shone like pearls when he opened his mouth.
He had brown crooked teeth.	His brown crooked teeth jutted out like fangs.
She had long red hair.	Her long red hair hung down in two long pigtails.
She had short black spiky hair.	Her thick black hair was short and spiked like a hedgehog.
His blonde hair was tangled.	His tangled blonde hair stuck up in all directions like a dandelion.
He had enormous hands.	Two enormous, shovel-like hands lifted her in the air.
Her hand was cold and bony.	Her bony hand felt as cold as a skeleton.
Her nails were dirty and claw-like.	Her dirty, claw-like nails tapped on the table.

15
Characters (heroes) – personality

NOUNS	ADJECTIVES
Personality, strengths, emotions **Joy**, happiness, delight **Bravery**, courage, determination **Excitement**, happiness, delight **Face**, expression	**Brave**, courageous, determined **Happy**, excited, delighted, beaming **Impish**, cheeky, mischievous **Funny**, amusing, humorous **Friendly**, caring, calm **Soft**, warm, gentle
Eyes	**Wide**, round **Bright**, clear, vivid, brilliant **Twinkling**, sparkling, glittering
Voice, tone **Smile**, grin, giggle, chuckle, laughter **Whisper**, murmur **Shout**, yell, scream	**Loud**, jolly, cheerful **Quiet**, low
Arms, hands, fingers, legs **Hug**, embrace **Dance**, jig **Clap**, wave	**Eager**, keen **Wild**, mad, lively, animated, energetic

15 *Characters: characters (heroes) – personality*

VERBS
Lit, shone, beamed **Danced**, sparkled, twinkled, gleamed
Said, spoke, shouted, squealed **Giggled**, laughed **Whispered**, murmured
Held, hugged, cuddled, snuggled, embraced **Waved**, shook, clapped
Skipped, danced, hopped, jigged **Crouched**, crawled, crept, walked, ran, sprinted

PHRASES (Nouns and Adjectives)	PHRASES (Verbs)
wide jolly face	beamed at her warmly
round friendly face	was very comforting
impish grin	spread over her face
eager smile	lit up his face
wide toothy grin	flashed across his face
dark brown eyes	twinkled impishly
bright green eyes	danced with excitement
huge grey eyes	twinkled with laughter
bright blue eyes	sparkled like diamonds
wide green eyes	were warm and friendly
grey eyes as big as saucers	lit up with excitement
loud excited shout	brought his mother running
impish giggle	made them laugh
smug grin like a Cheshire cat	appeared on his face
with a squeal of delight	she jumped up and down
with a whoop of excitement	he hopped up and down on the spot
with a broad grin on her face	she skipped along the path

SENTENCES	
Level 1	**Level 2**
He had a jolly face.	His wide, jolly face beamed at her warmly.
She had a friendly face.	Her round, friendly face was very comforting.
There was an impish grin on her face.	An impish grin spread over her face.
He had an angelic smile.	An eager, angelic smile lit up his face.
He had a toothy grin.	A wide, toothy grin flashed across his face.
She had twinkling brown eyes.	Her dark brown eyes twinkled impishly.
She had bright green eyes.	Her bright green eyes danced with excitement.
He had huge grey eyes.	His huge grey eyes twinkled with laughter.
Her eyes were as big as saucers.	Her grey eyes were as big as saucers and lit up with excitement.
He gave a loud, excited shout.	His loud, excited shout brought his mother running.
She had an impish giggle.	Her impish giggle made them laugh.
He had a smug grin.	A smug grin like a Cheshire cat spread across his face.
She squealed with delight.	With a squeal of delight, she jumped up and down.
He whooped with excitement.	With a whoop of excitement, he hopped up and down on the spot.
She had a broad grin on her face.	She skipped along the path with a broad grin on her face.

16
Characters (heroes) – animals

NOUNS	ADJECTIVES
Dog, puppy **Spaniel**, golden retriever **Wolf**	**Cute**, lovely, sweet, adorable, cuddly, loving **Beautiful**, stunning, gorgeous, magnificent **Friendly**, loyal **Happy**, contented **Playful**, cheeky, frisky, mischievous **Quiet**, noisy **Nosy**, curious **Shy**, timid
Cat, kitten	
Hamster, guinea pig, gerbil	
Horse, foal, pony **Unicorn**, Pegasus	
Elephant	
Fish, seahorse, dolphin	
Parrot, owl, Phoenix	
Body, tail **Wings** **Fins**, flippers **Head**, neck, shoulders **Face**, eyes, ears, nose **Mouth**, lips, tongue, teeth, cheeks, whiskers **Smile**, grin, yawn	**White**, brown, black, grey, green, blue, red, scarlet, pink, purple, golden, yellow, amber, golden, honey, rainbow-coloured, flame-coloured, brightly coloured **Spotty**, striped, patterned
	Long, short, stumpy **Thin**, narrow, beady **Wide**, broad, bulging
	Small, little, tiny, bat-sized **Big**, large, giant, huge, enormous, massive

Hair, body, skin, fur, feathers, scales	**Fluffy**, furry, hairy, wiry **Smooth**, soft, sleek, shiny, silky, velvety, glossy, gleaming **Rough**
Hands, fingers, paws **Legs**, arms, feet, hooves	**Front**, back, hind
	Fast, swift, energetic **Strong**, powerful **Incredible**, awesome **Slow**, delicate **Weak**, wobbly, unsteady
Claws, nails, talons	**Pointy**, sharp **Curved**
Whisper, hiss, grunt **Squeak**, whine, whimper, yelp **Laugh**, giggle, cackle, click, whistle **Purr**, meow, mew **Whinny**, neigh **Squawk**, shriek, hoot **Trumpet**, roar	**Loud**, booming **Quiet**, silent **High**, high-pitched, squeaky **Low**, deep **Excited** **Nervous**

VERBS
Covered, grew
Stroked, tickled, rubbed, brushed
Cuddled, hugged
Curled, nestled
Touched, pawed, nuzzled
Licked, groomed, nibbled
Clawed, scraped, clung **Dug**, burrowed
Sniffed, snuffled
Flicked, flickered, flapped, swished, swatted
Cocked, twitched
Looked, eyed, watched
Beamed, shone, sparkled, twinkled **Stared**, glared

16 *Characters: characters (heroes) – animals*

Called, announced
Woofed, grunted, growled, barked, howled
Cried, yelped, yipped, whimpered, squealed
Purred, meowed, mewed, hissed, squeaked
Neighed, whinnied, snorted
Rumbled, roared, trumpeted
Laughed, chuckled, cackled, clicked, whistled
Chirped, sang, spoke, imitated, mimicked **Hooted**, shrieked
Rocked, swayed, bobbed
Wobbled, waddled
Strutted, stalked
Walked, ambled, lumbered
Scrabbled, scrambled
Skipped, jumped, leaped, spun
Danced, pranced, frolicked
Ran, bounded, raced, scampered, scurried
Trotted, cantered, galloped
Bucked, reared, charged
Rose, lifted
Flew, glided, soared
Plunged, swooped, pounced
Swam, surfed, dived

PHRASES (Nouns and Adjectives)	PHRASES (Verbs)
cute, brown puppy	was a ball of fluff
adorable, white fluffy pup	cuddled into my arms
playful pup	was a bundle of energy and mischief
	rolled over onto his tummy
	clutched the soft toy between his front paws

curious puppy	buried her head in the basket
with rapid little snuffles	sniffed every object in the basket
playful spaniel	spun round and round chasing his tail
with a wide, cheeky grin	swooped on the trainer
with a big doggy smile	ran off with the shoe dangling from her mouth
small, curly white dog	jumped vertically up and down when he saw the lead
	yelped and yipped excitedly
friendly golden retriever	bounded up to them with a ball in her mouth
	wagged her tail excitedly
tiny front paws	scraped at the ground furiously
massive hairy paws	sent earth flying everywhere
coat of long, silky red hair	was covered in a sheet of icy water droplets
soaking wet dog	shook his coat
	sent a shower of freezing cold water all over us
with a wide yawn	flopped onto her side
	pressed her body against my leg
	curled up on my feet
a pair of wide, bulging brown eyes	stared out from under the chair
bright brown eyes	watched every bite I took
	followed every movement of my spoon
	eyed the bacon hopefully
with a low, deep growl	cocked an ear
	bounded to her feet
with a high-pitched whine	pawed at the door
giant black and brown dog	guarded the gate

PHRASES (Nouns and Adjectives)	PHRASES (Nouns and Adjectives)
snow-white kitten	was as round and fluffy as a cotton ball
tiny pink tongue	was as rough as sandpaper
	licked her front paw
	rubbed it over her cheeks and ears
	flicked around her lips
with a smug look on his face	licked his lips
with a deep, contented purr	rubbed against my ankles
	pounded her front paws on my leg
with a purr as loud as a drill	nestled in my lap
with a little squeaking noise	tucked his head under his paw
pointy little ears	twitched when she heard the snap of the lid on the sardine tin
bat-sized ears	flicked nervously at the sound of the panting dog
green eyes	flickered contentedly as I rubbed her under the chin
with a tail as straight as a rod	strutted out of the room
	stalked through the long grass
long thin whiskers	twitched as she eyed the mouse
tiny, needle-sharp teeth	nibbled delicately at the fur on her side
pair of wide, staring green eyes	stared out from under the bush
with his legs stretched out straight	landed on all four paws with ease
long sharp claws	dug into my trousers as she climbed up my leg
	scraped against the side of the sofa
with a high-pitched meow	leaped up onto the table
small honey-coloured body of the guinea pig	was partly hidden under a pile of shavings
white body	had black and red patches
long, thick silky brown fur	gleamed after it had been groomed
small silky head	nestled into my neck

little beady black eyes	searched for a place to hide
tiny furry ears	were stiff and straight up in the air
	pressed back against its head
guinea pig's tail	was a little bald stump
short, stocky legs	raced around the wheel as it spun quickly round and round
	scrabbled on the wooden floor
	scrambled up my jumper
front paws	waved in the air as he stood upright on his hind legs
large, sharp front teeth	gnawed at the bars of the cage
	nibbled my finger
bulging cheeks	were stuffed full of seeds
long, sharp claws	dug into my trousers as she shot down my leg
snow-white unicorn	leapt forwards into the air
with its long, powerful legs	took three enormous strides and leapt into the air
snow-white Pegasus	glided over the rooftops
	flew into the treetops
gleaming golden horn	spiralled from her forehead
massive white wings	unfurled like gigantic sails
	burst from between his shoulder blades
	flapped powerfully through the air
	flattened against his shoulders as he swooped to the ground
golden saddle	glittered on his back
stunning Palomino	had a shiny gold coat and a white mane and tail
black horse	had a white star on his forehead
frisky brown foal	threw her head back
	galloped after her mother
gentle grey horse	came up to the fence
	took the carrot daintily from my hand

long, swishing white tail	flicked across her back to get rid of the flies
stunning brown horse	let me jump onto her back
	took huge powerful strides as we galloped across the field
curious pony	blew on my hand
	nuzzled my hand to see if I had brought her anything
long, flowing mane	was like a thick rope to hold on to
beautiful gleaming black stallion	pricked his ears
	threw his head back and snorted
	raced around the paddock
	bucked and reared to unseat me
her upper lip	rolled back in a huge toothy smile
with an excited whinny	she trotted to the gate
her huge front hoof	lifted in the air
	stamped on the ice
enormous grey beast	lumbered towards me with huge flapping ears
	swayed from side to side
huge ears like sails	flapped against his body
long hairy swishing tail	swatted the flies away
thousands of deep wrinkles	covered her face
large, gentle brown eyes	were half-closed as I hosed her down
	were hidden in wrinkled folds
long grey trunk	snaked down
	brushed my cheek with its damp, gentle tip
	slowly uncurled to lower me to the ground
	rose in the air as she let out a loud trumpeting call
sleek grey body	glided towards me
	bobbed up and down in the water
grey triangular fin	sliced through the water towards me
curious dolphin	poked her head out of the water

friendly dolphin	announced her arrival with a series of clicks, whistles and squeaks
	swam to me
	had a beautiful smiling face
	looked me right in the eye
	rubbed against my legs
	nuzzled me in the ribs
excited dolphin	cackled with excitement
	danced on her tail
	leaped out of the water
	dived under the water
	jumped from wave to wave
brave dolphin	offered me her fin to hold onto
	dived underneath me
	caught one of my feet on her snout
	pushed me to the surface
huge, brightly coloured parrot	was a mixture of all colours of the rainbow
	had red, yellow, orange and purple feathers
	had a beautiful violet and sapphire head
small, noisy parrot	had a body as green as grass
	had black, red and blue tail feathers
enormous Phoenix	was as large as an eagle
	had golden wings
	had a neck of golden feathers
	glowed in a bed of hot ashes
	smelt of incense
flame-coloured Phoenix	fluffed its feathers in a dazzling display
	stretched its wings
	soared into the sky and burst into flames
tufts of velvety black feathers on top of his head	quivered as he bobbed up and down

immense black eyes	stared at me without blinking
	sparkled with intelligence
one beady black eye	opened wide and watched my every move
bright green head	tilted to one side as he gave me a curious stare
	bobbed up and down
bright yellow beak	picked at his feathers
long scarlet red beak	combed his feathers
	opened wide as it imitated my song
thin legs	landed on my outstretched arm
sharp curved claws	gripped on to the metal bar as she hung upside down from the roof
tiny body	rocked back and forth on his perch in time to the music
whirr of golden wings	as it flew into the air
rustle of feathers	as it tucked its beak under its wing

SENTENCES

Level 1	Level 2
The tiny brown puppy was very cute and fluffy.	The cute tiny brown puppy was a ball of fluff.
The white, fluffy pup was adorable.	The adorable, white fluffy pup cuddled into my arms.
The pup was very playful.	The playful pup was a bundle of energy and mischief.
The puppy was curious about all the new smells.	The curious puppy buried her head in the basket and sniffed every object in it.
The puppy spun round and round.	The playful puppy spun round and round chasing her tail.
The dog had a cheeky grin on its face.	With a wide, cheeky grin, the dog swooped on the trainer and ran off with it dangling in his mouth.
She had massive, hairy paws.	Her massive, hairy paws scraped at the ground and sent earth flying everywhere.
The dog was soaking wet.	The soaking wet dog shook his coat and sent a shower of freezing cold water all over us.

She yawned and flopped onto her side.	With a wide yawn, she flopped onto her side, then curled up on my feet.
He had bright brown eyes and wanted to have some of my bacon.	His bright, brown eyes eyed the bacon hopefully and watched every bite I took.
He whined and pawed at the door.	With a high-pitched whine, he pawed at the door to go out.
The kitten was as white as snow.	The snow-white kitten was as round and fluffy as a cotton ball.
She licked her front paw with her tiny pink tongue.	With her tiny pink tongue, she licked her front paw, rubbed it over her cheek, licked it again and then rubbed it over her ear.
He purred contentedly.	He leaped onto my lap and with a deep, contented purr, pounded his front paws on my leg.
Her purr was as loud as a drill.	With a purr as loud as a drill, she rubbed her head against my ankles.
He had pointy little ears.	His pointy little ears twitched when he heard the snap of the lid on the sardine tin.
Her tail stuck straight up in the air.	With a tail as straight as a rod, she strutted out of the room.
He hid under the bush.	A pair of wide, staring green eyes stared out from under the bush.
She scratched the side of the sofa.	Her long sharp claws scraped against the side of the sofa.
She meowed loudly.	With a high-pitched meow, she leaped up onto the table where her bowl was being filled.
The guinea pig hid under the shavings.	The small, honey-coloured body of the guinea pig was partly hidden under a pile of shavings.
The gerbil had a small, silky brown head.	The gerbil nestled its small, silky brown head into my neck.
She had short little legs.	She raced around the wheel on her short little legs as it spun quickly round and round.
He nibbled on my finger.	His large, sharp front teeth nibbled my finger.
Her cheeks were bulging.	Her plump, bulging cheeks were stuffed full of seeds.
She had very long, sharp claws.	Her long, sharp claws dug into my trousers as she shot down my leg.
The unicorn was snow white with a gleaming golden horn.	The snow-white unicorn leapt forwards into the air, its golden horn gleaming on its forehead.

The unicorn flew over the houses.	The unicorn took three enormous strides, leapt into the air and glided over the rooftops.
Pegasus had massive white wings.	Pegasus unfurled her white wings like gigantic sails and soared into the air.
Pegasus had a golden saddle on his back.	A golden saddle glittered from Pegasus' back.
The brown foal was very playful.	The frisky brown foal threw her head back and galloped after her mother.
The enormous brown horse was amazing.	The stunning brown horse let me jump onto her back and with huge powerful strides, she galloped across the field.
The pony was curious and searched my hand for something to eat.	The curious pony blew on my fingers and nuzzled my hand to see if I had brought her anything.
The black stallion was beautiful.	The beautiful black stallion pricked up his ears, threw his head back and raced around the paddock bucking and kicking.
She gave me a huge smile and showed me her enormous row of teeth.	Her upper lip rolled back in a huge toothy smile to reveal her enormous teeth.
She whinnied excitedly.	With an excited whinny, she trotted to the gate where I was waiting.
He stamped on the ice with his front hoof.	He lifted his huge front hoof in the air and stamped down on the ice.
There was an enormous grey beast coming towards me.	An enormous grey beast lumbered towards me with its huge ears like sails flapping against its body.
It had a long hairy tail.	Its long hairy swishing tail swatted the flies away.
The elephant had large, gentle brown eyes.	The elephant's large, brown eyes were half-closed as I hosed her down.
The elephant had a long, grey trunk.	The elephant's long, grey trunk snaked down to brush my cheek with its damp, gentle tip.
The elephant lowered me to the ground.	The elephant slowly uncurled its long, grey trunk and lowered me to the ground.
She raised her trunk and trumpeted.	She raised her trunk in the air and let out a loud trumpeting call.
I could see a grey fin coming through the water towards me.	A grey, triangular fin sliced through the water towards me.
The dolphin bobbed up and down in the water.	The sleek grey body of the dolphin bobbed up and down in the water.

The dolphin was very curious.	The curious dolphin poked her head out of the water and swam towards me.
The dolphin was friendly and smiled at me.	The friendly dolphin smiled at me and poked me in the ribs.
The dolphin was extremely excited.	The dolphin danced on her tail and cackled with excitement.
The brave dolphin rescued me from drowning.	The brave dolphin dived underneath me, caught one of my feet on her snout and pushed me to the surface. She offered me one of her fins to hold onto and took me to the dingy.
The Phoenix was red and as large as an eagle.	The enormous, flame-coloured Phoenix was as large as an eagle with huge golden wings.
The parrot was huge and was a mix of bright colours.	The huge, brightly coloured parrot was a mixture of all colours of the rainbow.
The small parrot had a green body and was very noisy.	The small, noisy parrot had a body as green as grass with black and red tail feathers.
The Phoenix flew into the air and burst into flames.	The flame-coloured Phoenix stretched its wings, soared into the sky and burst into flames.
The parrot bobbed his head up and down as he sat on the branch.	The tufts of velvety black feathers quivered as the parrot bobbed its head up and down.
The parrot opened an eye.	One beady black eye opened wide and watched my every move.
It had a bright yellow beak.	The parrot's bright yellow beak opened wide and its head bobbed up and down as it imitated my song.
The parrot loved music.	The parrot's tiny body rocked back and forth on his perch in time to the music.
It went to sleep with its beak under its wing.	There was a rustle of feathers as it tucked its beak under its wing.

17
Characters (villains) – personality

NOUNS	ADJECTIVES
Personality, weaknesses	**Cold**, evil, nasty, horrid, horrible **Mean**, jealous **Angry**, furious
Face, expression **Grin**, smirk, smile, sneer, sulk **Mouth**, lips, fangs	**Fierce**, scary, dangerous **Loud**, deafening, scary **High**, high-pitched **Creepy**, strange, sinister **Quiet**, low, ghostly
Voice, tone **Shout**, yell, roar, scream, screech **Whisper**, hiss, mutter **Snarl**, growl, bark	
Eyes, look **Stare**, glare	**Bloodshot** **Small**, buggy **Large**, wide, bulging, staring **Cold**, icy
Arms, hands, fingers, nails	**Long**, sharp, pointy, pointed, curved

VERBS
Plotted, planned, schemed
Looked, crossed, flashed, flitted, flickered **Spread**, stretched, covered **Smiled**, grinned, smirked, sneered **Clenched**, tightened, ground

Shouted, yelled, screamed, screeched
Whispered, hissed, muttered
Snarled, growled, barked, roared, bellowed

Stared, glared
Narrowed
Widened, bulged
Blinked, rolled

Grabbed, snatched, grasped
Held, gripped
Pushed, dragged, pulled, tugged, twisted
Pinched, scratched, slapped, thumped, kicked
Rubbed, pressed

PHRASES (Nouns and Adjectives)	PHRASES (Verbs)
sinister girl	plotted every move carefully
horrible, creepy man	schemed to steal the treasure from under our noses
dangerous, jealous enemy	planned to make us suffer for his defeat
evil, sneering expression	spread across her face
nasty smirk	crossed her face
sinister smile	stretched across her face
pale lips	were pressed into a tight, thin line
nasty hiss	sprayed from between her gritted teeth
deafening shout of fury	came from the other room
high-pitched screech	gave me a fright
horrible cold voice	made me duck behind the sofa
loud, sneering snarl	reminded me of a demonic monster
loud, raging shout	echoed around the building
low, quiet growl	warned me not to get any closer
huge black teeth	jutted out like fangs
cold sinister expression	threatened some evil punishment
thick flabby lips	twisted into a vicious snarl
thin lips	smirked evilly as she tied me to the chair
with a nasty grin on his face	he bellowed loudly for his assistant

cruel smirk	spread across her lips
high-pitched giggle	made a shiver charge down my spine
booming laugh	was evil, sinister and scary
quiet, ghostly whispers	made my skin crawl
fierce stare	made my legs tremble
small, buggy eyes	stared viciously at me
bloodshot eyes	stared at the map
dirty, gnarled fingers	dug painfully into my arm
long, pointy nails	were like sharpened claws
clenched fist	banged on the door
long, claw-like nails	tapped impatiently on the table

SENTENCES

Level 1	Level 2
The girl was cold and sinister.	The sinister girl plotted every move carefully.
The man was horrible and creepy.	The horrible, creepy man schemed to steal the treasure from under our noses.
His jealousy made him a dangerous enemy.	His jealously had turned him into a dangerous enemy who was planning to make us suffer for his defeat.
She had an evil expression on her face.	An evil, sneering expression spread across her face.
There was a sinister smile on her face.	A sinister smile stretched across her face.
There was an angry look on his face.	An angry look flashed across his face.
She had pale, thin lips.	Her pale, dry lips were pressed together in a tight, thin line.
He looked at me with a hostile expression.	He stared at me with a hostile expression as he plotted what to do next.
She hissed at me nastily.	A nasty hiss sprayed from between her gritted teeth.
There was a loud, furious shout.	A loud, furious shout came from the other room.
She heard a high-pitched screech.	The high-pitched screech gave her a fright.

He had a horrible, cold voice.	I heard his horrible, cold voice and ducked quickly behind the sofa.
Her loud, sneering snarl scared me.	Her loud, sneering snarl terrified me as it reminded me of a demonic monster.
He gave a quiet, low growl.	He uttered a quiet, low growl that warned me not to get any closer.
Her huge teeth jutted out like fangs.	As she snarled, she bared her huge, yellow teeth that jutted out like fangs.
A cold, sinister expression spread over her face.	Her cold, sinister expression threatened some evil punishment.
He had thick, flabby lips.	His thick, flabby lips twisted into a snarl.
Her thin lips smirked evilly.	Her thin lips smirked evilly as she tied me to the chair.
He had a nasty grin on his face.	With a nasty grin on his face, he bellowed for his assistant.
She smirked at me.	A cruel smirk spread across her lips as she watched me struggling to get free.
His high-pitched giggle turned into wild, hysterical laughter.	His high-pitched giggle soon turned into wild, hysterical laughter and made a shiver charge down my spine.
He had an evil, booming laugh.	He gripped the weapon in both hands and uttered an evil, sinister laugh that boomed down the hall.
I heard quiet, ghostly whispers outside the door.	The quiet, ghostly whispers coming from outside the door made my skin crawl and my palms sweaty.
His fierce stare terrified me.	His fierce stare made my legs tremble.
He had small, buggy eyes.	He stared at me with his small, buggy eyes.
She had large, bulging green eyes.	Her large, bulging green eyes filled me with terror.
His eyes were tiny and bloodshot.	His tiny, bloodshot eyes stared at my injured arm.
Her fingers were dirty and gnarled.	Her dirty, gnarled fingers dug painfully into my arm.
She had long, pointy nails like claws.	Her long, pointy nails grabbed my hand like sharpened claws.
She tapped impatiently on the table with her long fingernails.	Her long, needle-sharp nails tapped impatiently on the table as she waited for my answer.
He clenched his fist.	He banged menacingly on the door with his clenched fist.

18
Characters (villains) – animals

NOUNS	ADJECTIVES
Animals: **Crocodile**, snake, alligator **Wolf**, dog, hyena **Bull**, boar, camel **Lion**, tiger, cheetah **Porcupine** **Spider**, scorpion, cockroach **Wasp**, mosquito, bee **Shark**, squid, crab **Dragon,** werewolf	*Personality/appearance:* **Grumpy**, creepy, sly, cunning **Evil**, wicked, cruel, vicious **Fierce**, dangerous, deadly **Scary**, terrifying **Ugly**, vile, hideous
	Colour/pattern: **Green**, emerald, grey, black, dark, red, yellow, amber, coppery, brass **Spotty**, stripy, scarred
Body Parts: **Body**, tail **Head**, horns **Legs**, feet, hooves **Arms**, wings, tentacles, fins **Eyes**	*Size:* **Big**, large, huge, enormous, gigantic **Tiny**, small **Long**, short
Nose, snout **Mouth**, tongue **Hands**, fingers	*Shape:* **Wide**, broad **Narrow** **Bent**, curved, forked
	Speed: **Quick**, fast, swift **Slow**, lumbering

Covering:	*Covering:*
Skin, fur, hair, scales, quills, armour **Mane**, beard	**Scaly**, smooth, shiny, furry, hairy, bony **Slimy**, slippery **Thick**, tough **Dirty**, filthy, tangled, shaggy
Weapons:	*Weapons:*
Teeth, tongue, fangs **Nails**, claws, talons **Spots**, warts **Poison**, venom, slime, spit, saliva, mucus, pus	**Sharp**, needle-sharp, pointed, jagged, forked **Poisonous**, venomous **Purple**, blue, silver, yellow, cream **Bulging**, oozing, trailing, drooling
Smell, stink, stench, odour	**Smelly**, stinky, awful, horrible, disgusting, revolting
Hiss, growl, howl, scream, shriek, screech	**Loud**, booming, deafening **High**, high-pitched **Low**, quiet, menacing

VERBS
Covered, grew, sprouted **Hung**, drooped, trailed
Oozed, dribbled, bulged
Stared, looked, glared, glinted
Grinned, smiled, sneered
Hissed, growled, whispered, snarled, snapped **Screeched**, shrieked, cried, roared, bellowed
Sharpened, scratched, scraped **Grabbed**, lunged, snatched, grasped
Crawled, crept, sneaked, stalked, slithered, scampered **Flew**, flapped, fluttered, soared, swooped
Attacked, pecked, pinched, beat, slammed, smashed **Thrashed**, whipped, ripped, tore, crushed, trapped
Ate, drank
Sprayed, squirted, belched

18 *Characters: characters (villains) – animals*

PHRASES (Nouns and Adjectives)	PHRASES (Verbs)
monster, part eagle and part scorpion	was hidden in the trees
creature with the body of a lizard and the head of a giant wasp	scuttled towards us
enormous, ugly, three-legged bird	grabbed my leg
gigantic, red, furry spider with long purple spikes	reared up in front of me
striped red and green boar	was as quick as lightning
giant yellow stripy cockroach	flew into the air
tough, green, scaly skin	covered its body like armour
emerald scales	bulged from its body
thick, tangled grey fur	covered its feet
huge deadly porcupine quills	sprouted from its head
shiny coppery feathers	covered its body
bright purple skin	hung like a sack from its neck
long, snarling face	stared viciously back at me from the top of the rock
creepy, dark eyes	glinted from its terrifying hyena head
one enormous bloodshot eye	glared at us from the centre of its head
long, hairy arms like a gorilla	smashed everything in its path
huge, hairy fist	slammed into the boulder
long, spear-like tail	whipped from side to side
silver spiral horn	sprouted from its furry head like a dagger
red eagle wings	sprouted from its shoulders
big curved, jagged beak	ripped a hole in the wall
long, jagged claws	sharpened into deadly points on the rocks
hooked claws	scratched huge marks in the tree
long thin snout	filled with pointed tentacles
terrifying tentacles	lunged through the water
huge blue tongue	hung from its monstrous slobbering mouth
long, forked tongue	flicked in and out searching for its prey
enormous red tongue	lolled out of the side of its mouth

poisonous black slime	dribbled from its needle-sharp teeth
long, slimy strands of green mucus	oozed from its huge black nose
vile, yellow poison	flew into the air
purple slime	oozed from the huge warts on its feet
venomous strings of green saliva	hung from its mouth
slimy black spit	flew from its snapping jaws
creamy green mucus	belched from its huge flared nostrils
bulging yellow warts	squirted deadly poison
poison from the warts on its feet	smelt of rotting fish
crusty slime on its jaw	stank of sweaty seaweed
revolting stench	sprayed from its tail
werewolf's breath	smelt of mouldy cheese
fierce, menacing hiss	burst through its bared teeth
high-pitched screech	ripped through the darkness
hideous grin on its face	as it prepared to attack
thunderous hooves	pounded through the forest

SENTENCES

Level 1	Level 2
The monster was part eagle and part scorpion.	A monster, part eagle and part scorpion, was hidden in the trees.
The creature had the body of a lizard and the head of a giant wasp.	A creature with the body of a lizard and the head of a giant wasp scuttled towards us.
It was an enormous, ugly, three-legged bird.	An enormous, ugly, three-legged bird grabbed my leg.
It was a gigantic, red, furry spider with long purple spikes.	A gigantic, red, furry spider with long purple spikes reared up in front of me.
There was a striped red and green boar.	The striped red and green boar was as quick as lightning.
I saw a giant yellow stripy cockroach.	I watched the giant yellow stripy cockroach fly into the air.
It had tough, green scaly skin all over its body.	Tough, green scaly skin covered its body like armour.

It had huge porcupine quills on its head.	Huge, deadly porcupine quills sprouted from its head.
There were shiny red feathers all over its body.	Shiny coppery feathers covered its body.
It had bright purple skin around its neck.	Bright purple skin hung like a sack around its neck.
It had a long, snarling face.	Its long, snarling face stared viciously back at me from the top of the rock.
It had a hyena head and creepy, dark eyes.	Its creepy, dark eyes glinted from its terrifying hyena head.
It had one enormous eye.	One enormous eye glared at us from the centre of its head.
It had long, hairy arms like a gorilla.	It had long, hairy arms like a gorilla that smashed everything in its path.
It had a long tail like a spear.	Its long, spear-like tail whipped from side to side.
It had a big curved beak.	Its big, curved, jagged beak ripped a hole in the wall.
Its claws were long and sharp.	Its long, jagged claws had been sharpened into deadly points on the rocks.
It had a huge blue tongue and monstrous mouth.	A huge blue tongue hung from its monstrous, slobbering mouth.
It had a long, forked tongue like a snake.	Its long, forked tongue flicked in and out searching for its prey.
Its enormous red tongue hung out of its mouth.	Its enormous red tongue lolled out of the side of its mouth.
There was poisonous black slime on its teeth.	Poisonous black slime dribbled from its needle-sharp teeth.
There were long strands of green snot on its nose.	Long, slimy strands of green mucus oozed from its huge black nose.
It had huge warts on its feet.	Purple slime oozed from the huge warts on its feet.
It had bulging yellow warts all over its body.	The bulging yellow warts squirted deadly poison from all over its body.
It smelt of rotting fish.	The poison from the warts on its feet smelt of rotting fish.
It stank of sweaty seaweed.	The crusty slime on its jaw stank of sweaty seaweed.
It smelt of mouldy cheese.	The werewolf's breath smelt of mouldy cheese.

It hissed fiercely through its teeth.	A fierce, menacing hiss burst through its bared teeth.
There was a high-pitched screech.	A high-pitched screech ripped through the darkness.
There was a hideous grin on its face.	It grinned hideously as it prepared to attack.
I could hear its hooves thundering through the forest.	Its thunderous hooves pounded through the forest.

19
Defeating a villain

SETTING THE SCENE ...

★ Once upon a time ...
★ In a faraway land ...
★ A long time ago ...
★ Just last week ...
★ The wind was howling ...
★ You won't believe what happened to me ...
★ It sounds crazy, but it's true ...
★ I remember everything like it happened yesterday ...
★ It was a bright, sunny day ...

MOVING THE ACTION FORWARD ...

★ Then everything changed ...
★ Clouds blocked out the sun ...
★ After days of travelling ...
★ Finally, I arrived at ...
★ Hours later ...
★ After many hours ...
★ Soon after ...

CHANGING THE TIME OF DAY ...

★ Later that day ...
★ That evening ...
★ As night arrived ...

★ The following morning …
★ When I woke up …
★ It was getting dark …
★ After breakfast …

TIME CONJUNCTIONS …

★ First,
★ Firstly,
★ Then,
★ Next,
★ After that,
★ Afterwards,
★ Later,
★ Just then,
★ Before long,
★ Meanwhile,
★ Just at that moment,
★ Seconds later,

ACTION SCENE …

★ At once,
★ Instantly,
★ Without warning,
★ Quickly,
★ At the same time,
★ All of a sudden,
★ I had to …
★ Wasting no time, I …
★ I grabbed my …
★ Using all my strength, I …
★ Suddenly, I …
★ Straight away, I …
★ I needed my …
★ I saw her/him/it …
★ As I watched, she/he/it …
★ At that moment, she/he/it …
★ She/He/It swiftly …
★ Already she/he/it was …
★ She/He/It had hold of …
★ Without warning she/he/it …

19 *Characters: defeating a villain*

- ★ Put my ear to …
- ★ Listened for the sound of …
- ★ Peered out from behind …
- ★ Stared at the …
- ★ Tugged on the …
- ★ Slipped through the gap between …
- ★ Stopped dead in my tracks
- ★ Glanced over my shoulder
- ★ Darted through the …
- ★ Crouched on all fours behind …
- ★ Flung myself down behind …
- ★ Dived for cover under …
- ★ Sprinted across the …
- ★ Darted and dodged between the …
- ★ Swayed out of the way of its …
- ★ Leaped over the …
- ★ Sprang to my feet
- ★ …was closing in on me
- ★ Slammed my boot into …
- ★ Rolled underneath the …
- ★ Smashed a rock onto its …
- ★ Released an arrow
- ★ Found its mark in the centre of its forehead
- ★ Waved my sword
- ★ Lashed at its tentacles
- ★ Smashed its beak with my shield
- ★ Skewered the serpent with my dagger

ENDING THE ACTION …

- ★ After it was over,
- ★ Finally,
- ★ In the end,
- ★ Once outside,
- ★ Leaving that place behind,
- ★ The sky had brightened …
- ★ Eventually,
- ★ At last,
- ★ Ever since,
- ★ After all of that,
- ★ I was so relieved …
- ★ Behind me …

- ★ A little further on I …
- ★ After a while I …
- ★ I breathed a sigh of relief …
- ★ Next to me …
- ★ I was holding …
- ★ With a smile on my face …
- ★ I felt …
- ★ I had done it, I …

20
Dialogue

whispered	muttered	mumbled	sighed	gasped
babbled	cried	sobbed	moaned	wailed
howled	called	shouted	growled	snarled
roared	screeched	shrieked	begged	pleaded
asked	argued	questioned	challenged	told
declared	ordered	demanded	agreed	confirmed
replied	explained	repeated	giggled	chuckled
laughed	hooted	joked	teased	mocked
lied	denied	boasted	bragged	greeted
cheered	praised	repeated	chanted	echoed

USING AN ACTION WITH DIALOGUE

- ★ … she cried, as she ran from the room.
- ★ … he whispered while shaking his head.
- ★ … the girl shouted, slamming her fist on the desk.
- ★ … he called over his shoulder.
- ★ … she remarked, then flicked her hair.
- ★ … the man questioned while rubbing his chin.
- ★ … the woman announced, with a huge smile on her face.
- ★ … he muttered grimly, then stomped off.
- ★ … she mumbled under her breath and clenched her fists.
- ★ … the boy roared, stamping his feet.

★ … he replied with a shrug.

★ … the lady whimpered, clasping her hands together.

★ … he claimed, nodding his head quickly.

★ … she revealed, putting her hands out to encourage them to look closer.

★ … the man growled, walking towards them slowly.

★ … she gasped, with her hands over her mouth.

★ … he agreed, nodding his head several times.

★ … the girl wailed and threw herself onto the floor.

★ … the boy told them all, blushing.

USING ADVERBS WITH DIALOGUE

★ … she chanted wildly.

★ … he moaned softly.

★ … the woman lied loudly and confidently.

★ … the boy blurted suddenly.

★ … she teased repeatedly.

★ … the girl demanded firmly, with narrowed eyes.

★ … he echoed her voice mockingly.

★ … she bragged noisily to everyone.

★ … he declared proudly.

Part 3
Resources for 'Language in action'

A. 'THE NINJABREAD GIRL' BY ADAM BUSHNELL

Chapter 21 'The Ninjabread Girl' by Adam Bushnell

Chapter 22 Modelled sentences

Chapter 23 Innovating sentences model

Chapter 24 Coordination and subordination

B. 'CAPTAIN MOODY' AND HIS PIRATE CREW BY ADAM BUSHNELL

Chapter 25 'Captain Moody' and his pirate crew by Adam Bushnell

Chapter 26 Modelled sentences

Chapter 27 Innovating sentences model

Chapter 28 Coordination and subordination

C. 'RUBY RED' BY ALISON WILCOX

Chapter 29 'Ruby Red' by Alison Wilcox

Chapter 30 Modelled sentences

Chapter 31 Innovating sentences model

Chapter 32 Coordination and subordination

D. 'JACK AND THE CRYSTAL FANG' BY ALISON WILCOX

Chapter 33 'Jack and the Crystal Fang' by Alison Wilcox

Chapter 34 Modelled sentences

Chapter 35 Innovating sentences model

Chapter 36 Coordination and subordination

21

'The Ninjabread Girl'

Once upon a time there was a Ninjutsu trainer who decided to make a Gingerbread Girl. He gave her currants for eyes and cherries for her buttons. Then he gave her a black liquorice suit.

The Ninjutsu trainer put the Gingerbread Girl into the oven to bake.

When the smell of gingerbread filled the kitchen, the Ninjutsu trainer opened the oven door. Out leapt the Gingerbread Girl with a 'Hiiiiii-yaaaaa!'

The Gingerbread Girl ran straight past her maker and with a kick and a jump, leapt straight through an open window then out into the garden.

'Run! Run! So fast like a twirl … you can't catch me, I'm the Ninjabread Girl!'

The Ninjutsu trainer chased the Ninjabread Girl across the garden and down into the lane.

Just then she ran into a big, bad crocodile, who said, 'Stop! Stop! I want to eat you up!'

'Run! Run! So fast like a twirl … you can't catch me, I'm the Ninjabread Girl!' replied the little ninja.

The crocodile began to chase the Ninjabread Girl along with the Ninjutsu trainer.

The Ninjabread Girl ran on a little further and met a huge, angry wolf who said, 'Stop! Stop! I want to eat you up!'

'Run! Run! So fast like a twirl … you can't catch me, I'm the Ninjabread Girl!' replied the little ninja.

The wolf joined the crocodile and the Ninjutsu trainer chasing the Ninjabread Girl.

But she ran on further still until she met a massive, evil dragon, who said, "Stop! Stop! I want to eat you up!"

'Run! Run! So fast like a twirl … you can't catch me, I'm the Ninjabread Girl!' replied the little ninja.

The dragon, the wolf, the crocodile and the Ninjutsu trainer all chased the Ninjabread Girl down the lane.

She ran on even further until she came to a river.

'Oh no!' cried the Ninjabread Girl, 'My training is not yet complete! I cannot yet walk on water, nor can I turn invisible! What will I do? They will catch me!'

Just then, Kitsune, the fox spirit, came along and said, 'Jump upon my tail. I shall swim you across the river.'

'Do you promise not to eat me?' asked the Ninjabread Girl.

'Of course, I just want to help,' smiled Kitsune.

The Ninjabread Girl climbed onto Kitsune's tail. But soon the little ninja began to get wet.

'Climb onto my back,' said Kitsune.

So, the Ninjabread Girl did.

As they swam Kitsune said, 'You are too heavy. I am tired. Jump onto my nose.'

The Ninjabread Girl jumped onto Kitsune's nose!

No sooner had they reached the other side, Kitsune tossed the Ninjabread Girl up in the air. He opened his mouth and 'Snap!' That was the end of the Ninjabread Girl!

22
Modelled sentences

A. STORY PLOT

Simple statements

- ★ A Ninjitsu trainer made a Gingerbread Girl.
- ★ The Gingerbread girl ran away.
- ★ She said she was a Ninjabread Girl.
- ★ A crocodile tried to eat her.
- ★ A wolf tried to eat her.
- ★ A dragon tried to eat her.
- ★ She came to a river.
- ★ She could not cross it.
- ★ Kitsune, a fox spirit, took her across the river.
- ★ Kitsune ate the Ninjabread Girl.

B. QUESTIONS, EXCLAMATIONS AND COMMANDS

Questions

- ★ 'What will I do?'
- ★ 'Do you promise not to eat me?' asked the Ninjabread Girl.

Exclamations

- ★ 'Hiiiiii-yaaaaa!'
- ★ 'So fast like a twirl … you can't catch me, I'm the Ninjabread Girl!'
- ★ 'I want to eat you up!'
- ★ 'Oh no!'
- ★ 'My training is not yet complete! I cannot yet walk on water, nor can I turn invisible!'
- ★ 'Snap!'
- ★ That was the end of the Ninjabread Girl!

Commands

- ★ '**Run!**'
- ★ '**Stop! Stop!** I want to eat you up!'
- ★ '**Jump** upon my tail.'
- ★ '**Climb** onto my back,' said Kitsune.
- ★ '**Jump** onto my nose.'

C. DESCRIPTION: EXPANDED NOUN PHRASES, PREPOSITION PHRASES, DIALOGUE AND ALLITERATION

Expanded noun phrases

- ★ He gave her a **black liquorice suit**.
- ★ She ran into a **big, bad crocodile**.
- ★ She met a **huge, angry wolf**.
- ★ She ran on further until she met a **massive, evil dragon**.

Preposition phrases

- ★ The Ninjutsu trainer put the Gingerbread Girl **into the oven**.
- ★ She leapt straight **through an open window** then **out into the garden**.
- ★ He chased the Ninjabread Girl **across the garden** and **down into the lane**.
- ★ They all chased the Ninjabread Girl **down the lane**.
- ★ She ran on until she came **to a river**.
- ★ She jumped **onto Kitsune's tail**.
- ★ She jumped **onto Kitsune's nose**.
- ★ Kitsune tossed the Ninjabread Girl **up in the air**.

Dialogue

- ★ Just then she ran into a crocodile, who said, '**Stop! Stop! I want to eat you up!**'
- ★ '**Run! Run! So fast like a twirl … you can't catch me, I'm the Ninjabread Girl!**' replied the little ninja.
- ★ The Ninjabread Girl ran on a little further and met a wolf who said, '**Stop! Stop! I want to eat you up!**'
- ★ '**Run! Run! So fast like a twirl … you can't catch me, I'm the Ninjabread Girl!**' replied the little ninja.
- ★ But she ran on further still until she met a dragon, who said, '**Stop! Stop! I want to eat you up!**'
- ★ Just then, Kitsune, the fox spirit, came along and said, '**Jump upon my tail. I shall swim you across the river.**'
- ★ '**Do you promise not to eat me?**' asked the Ninjabread Girl.

★ '**Of course, I just want to help**.' smiled Kitsune.

★ '**Climb onto my back**,' said Kitsune.

★ As they swam Kitsune said, '**You are too heavy. I am tired. Jump onto my nose**.'

Alliteration

★ **w**alk on **w**ater

23
Innovating sentences model

STATEMENTS				
A	**Ninjitsu trainer**	**made a**	**Gingerbread Girl.**	
A		made a		.
The	**Gingerbread Girl**	**ran**	**away.**	
The		ran	away.	
She	**called herself**	**the**	**Ninjabread Girl.**	
She	called herself	the		.
A	**crocodile**	**tried**	**to eat her.**	
A		tried	to eat her.	
She	**came**	**to**	**a river.**	
She	came	to		.
She	**could not**	**cross it.**		
She	could not			.
She	**met a**	**fox spirit**	**called Kitsune.**	
She	met a		called .	
He	**took her**	**across the river.**		
He	took her			.
He	**ate**	**the Ninjabread Girl.**		
He	ate			

100

QUESTIONS		
Do	**you promise not to**	**eat me?**
Do	you promise not to	?

EXPANDED NOUN PHRASES				
He	**gave her a**	**black**	**liquorice**	**suit.**
He	gave her a			suit.
She	**met a**	**big**	**bad**	**crocodile.**
She	met a			.
She	**met a**	**huge**	**angry**	**wolf.**
She	met a			.
She	**met a**	**massive**	**evil**	**dragon.**
She	met a			.

PREPOSITIONS		
She	**ran**	**out of the garden.**
She		.
She	**ran**	**down the lane.**
She		.
She	**ran**	**until she came**	**to a river.**
She		until she came	.
She	**jumped**	**onto Kitsune's nose.**
She		.
He	**threw her**	**up in the air.**
He		.

24
Coordination and subordination

Clause (1)	Conjunction	Clause (2)	√
She is the Ninjabread Girl	**and**	a. she likes to tease others.	
		b. she is quite cheeky.	
The Ninjabread Girl can jump and kick	**but**	a. she cannot walk on water.	
		b. she doesn't escape the fox.	
She can be sneaky	**because**	a. she can turn invisible.	
		b. she can hide in the shadows with her black suit.	
She is a fast runner	**so**	a. she is hard to catch.	
		b. no one can keep up with her.	

EXERCISE 1: COMBINING THE PHRASES INTO SENTENCES AND INTO A PARAGRAPH

Using *and, but, because* and *so* to develop sentence structure
Complete the following sentence stems:

She is the Ninjabread Girl **and** _____

The Ninjabread Girl can jump and kick **but** _____

She can be sneaky **because** _____

She is a fast runner, **so** _____

Examples

She is the Ninjabread Girl **and** she likes to tease others.

The Ninjabread Girl can jump and kick **but** she doesn't escape the fox.

She can be sneaky **because** she can turn invisible.

She is a fast runner, **so** no one can keep up with her.

25

'Captain Moody and his pirate crew'

THE MAP

Chris had always longed for adventure. Ever since he was a boy, he had dreamed of being a knight. Or a superhero. Or a dragon trainer. Something that would make his life exciting.

Instead he was a fisherman. Every day he would row in his little boat across the sea and send his line into the water. Then he would wait … and wait … and wait. It was so boring! Sometimes, something exciting would happen like he would catch a crab instead of a fish. Or even catch something unusual like an old boot.

One day, Chris had rowed his boat over the calm and still sea. He was sitting holding his fishing rod when he felt it catch on something. It was probably caught on a jagged rock. He pulled and pulled but the line was stuck. Chris was about to cut the line with his penknife when he fell backwards.

'Ooof!'

He sat back up and reeled in the line. There, right on the end of his hook, was a bottle. It was old and dirty with a wooden stopper in the top. Chris pulled it free with a loud popping sound. He peered inside. There was a rolled up piece of paper. With slightly shaking hands, Chris pulled it out. He uncurled the paper and stared at it.

The Forest of Doom was marked on there. So was the Volcano of Death. There were other places too: the Swamp of Stink, the River of Evil, the Waterfall of Terror, the Lake of Madness and finally the Cave of Monsters. Right next to this last place was a bright red X.

Chris stood up quickly, making the boat wobble. He had a treasure map! He decided right then and there to become not a knight or a superhero or a dragon trainer but instead a … pirate!

'Yar!' he said, as he thought that was what a pirate might have said.

THE CREW

Chris rowed the boat back to the harbour as fast as he could. His mind was racing. He wouldn't just be any pirate. He would be the captain. He had the map after all. He needed new smart clothes as captains always seemed to dress quite nicely. He needed a tricorn hat to show he was the boss. He needed a cutlass and a flintlock pistol as he wouldn't take any nonsense from his crew. Crew! Where would he find a crew? Where would he find a ship?

As he tied his boat to the pier, Chris spotted a huge ship approaching the harbour. It had the figurehead of a pirate and the familiar black flag with a skull and crossed bones.

'Pirates!' Chris gasped.

He sprinted to the tailor's and bought a new jacket and hat. Then he raced to the black-smith for a sword and a gun. Once fully dressed as a pirate captain he ran back to the harbour.

Chris suddenly stopped. The ship had docked and the pirates on board were all carrying their captain.

'Call yourself a captain?' one pirate roared, 'You haven't found us any treasure for ages!'

'Throw him in the sea!' another bellowed, 'Feed him to the sharks!'

'Get rid of him!' a third cried, 'We need a new captain!'

Chris stopped. He watched the unfortunate pirate captain land with a mighty splash in the water. He then swam wildly away from the ship and the other pirates as fast as he could.

Chris gulped and walked slowly toward the ship.

'Ahoy there!' he cried feeling that he was really getting the hang of this pirate talk, 'If you need a new captain, then I'm your man … Yar!'

The pirates on the ship looked at him as he approached. Chris gulped again.

THE FLAG

'What's your name then?' one pirate asked.

'My name is Christopher Moody, but you can call me *Captain Moody!*'

The pirates looked him up and down.

'Your clothes look brand new!' another commented, 'What ships have you sailed on?'

'Erm … the *Good Ship Betty* … Yar!'

'Never heard of it,' a third laughed, 'What makes you think we'd be your crew?'

'Because I have this!'

Chris pulled the treasure map dramatically from his belt. The crew all stared at it wide eyed.

'We're your crew!' they chorused together.

Chris beamed and asked:

'What be your names … Yar!'

'I'm Stinky Sid,' one pirate replied.

'I'm Peg Leg Pete,' another answered.

'I'm Mad Mary,' a third cried.

The fourth member of the crew was lowering the ship's flag.

'I'm Tina Tailor and I'll make us a new flag!'

'Yeah, a better one than last time,' Stinky Sid said, 'Let's put stuff like unicorns, butterflies and kittens on this time.'

The pirates all looked at him.

'No,' Chris said firmly. 'I want it to be as red as blood and covered in piratey things like skulls and swords!'

Tina Tailor went below deck to make the flag straight away. Chris had a crew, and adventure was not far away.

THE JOURNEY

Chris studied the map and pointed to the north. The red flag with a golden skull, white sword and blue hourglass timer flapped in the wind. The sky was darkening, and the sea turned from blue to grey. Clouds gathered above like a flock of black sheep.

The island was not too far from the mainland. But Chris knew that with the approaching storm it was not going to be easy. Soon, waves were beating the sides of the ship. Rain lashed at them from above. The wind became a howling monster that lashed at them from all around.

Chris held tightly to the ship's wheel and tried to look brave. The other pirates clung on for dear life. Somehow, with lots of luck, and even more rum, they did it.

They were through the storm and saw the island on the horizon. The weather changed almost instantly. The sea was now calm and still. The clouds cleared into wisps of white fluff.

The ship sailed slowly into a shallow reef. The water here was emerald green. Rainbow-coloured fish darted between red, leafy coral.

'Gather around, crew!' Chris commanded.

The pirates closed in around the map.

'Let's park there at the top!' declared Chris, pointing at the Cave of Monsters with the red X.

'What?' cried the crew, clearly appalled.

'What's wrong?' asked Chris.

'You don't *park* a ship,' growled Stinky Sid.

'You don't go straight to the X either!' snarled Peg Leg Pete.

'You have to go to each place first!' barked Mad Mary.

'That's the pirate way!' shouted Tina Tailor.

Chris shrugged and thought it best to just say, 'Yar!'

THE ISLAND

The pirates dropped the anchor to the south of the small tropical island. The beach was empty, and the island looked deserted. The Forest of Doom was just beyond the beach. It was wild and overgrown. That would be their first stop.

They lowered a boat into the water and Stinky Sid rowed the crew to the beach. The golden sandy beach had powdery sand. The pirates followed Chris as he passed palm trees with huge leaves like a fan.

The Forest of Doom was a terrifying place. The moment the crew entered they were freezing cold. Gone were the tropical waters, sandy beach and blazing sunshine. Instead a cold wind crept through the forest. White human and animal bones were scattered all around. Skeletons, skulls and jawbones littered the forest floor.

A roaring sound in the distance made the trees shake slightly and the pirates shake even more.

'Erm, pirate crew?'

They grabbed hold of him.

'Yes, Captain?' they chorused together.

'So, this is the Forest of Doom. Then we need to go to the Volcano of Death, the Swamp of Stink, the River of Evil, the Waterfall of Terror, the Lake of Madness and finally the Cave of Monsters.'

The pirates all nodded.

'Or we could just park at the top of the island and go straight to the X.'

The pirates all nodded even more.

Then they were off. The crew raced back to the golden sandy beach and leapt into the rowing boat. Stinky Sid rowed over a stunning, rainbow-coloured coral reef that lay beneath the surface of the water. Then they climbed a rope ladder, back to the safety of the ship.

THE MONSTER

The Cave of Monsters was at the northern tip of the island. Here high rocks rose vertically out of the sea. Chris had to carefully steer the ship to drop the anchor. Stinky Sid rowed the boat slowly past huge, jagged rocks that guarded the island. The grey tip of a shark's fin sliced through the water nearby.

Eventually, they made it to the shore. The beach here was scattered with objects from an ancient shipwreck. The battered remains of ships were strewn about here and there.

The cave was ahead of them. According to the map, the treasure chest was buried under rocks just inside the cave. Chris stepped forward and peered at the cave's entrance. A skeleton of an enormous creature blocked the mouth of the cave. The bones were bleached white from the sun.

'Maybe this is the monster?' Stinky Sid said, uncertainly.

'So, it's dead!' grinned Peg Leg Pete.

'Let's just go in and get the treasure then!' smiled Mad Mary.

'Isn't it the Cave of Monsters?' asked Tina Tailor, 'As in plural?'

Chris drew his cutlass just at the moment the monster burst from darkness of the cave. It had the head of a shark, the tentacles of an octopus, a shell like a turtle, the claws of a lobster and the tail of a stingray. It towered above the pirate crew and roared a terrible roar. It gnashed its teeth, snapped its claws and crawled towards them. The octopus tentacles coiled over every rock as it approached.

Chris and his crew turned to run back to the boat. But the monster leapt up into the air and landed with a splat on the beach. It blocked their way of escape. It was either run away or fight. Chris pulled free his flintlock pistol and watched his crew scream, then run in terror.

They hid in the cave. Chris was on his own.

THE BATTLE

Chris held the sword in one hand and the gun in the other. His hands were shaking, and his knees were knocking.

Suddenly, the monster roared again and began to creep towards him. Wasting no time, Chris aimed and shot his flintlock pistol … and missed. Without warning, the creature stretched out a long, slithering tentacle and grabbed him. It brought him close to the snapping jaws that dripped saliva noisily onto the rocks below. Wasting no time, Chris sliced with his sword. The blade swung past the monster's shark-tip nose, missing it by millimetres. At that very moment, the monster brought up a claw to snap at Chris's neck. Not a moment too soon, he sliced again with the sword and cut the hard skin of the claw.

The monster howled loudly and dropped Chris with a thud. Using another claw to support the one that had been injured, it scuttled rapidly into the water. It disappeared under the surface of the water and darted away.

Chris jumped up to his feet to see the pirate crew applauding madly from the entrance of the cave. He ran to join them and peered into the darkness.

There was a huge wooden treasure chest towards the back. The crew raced over, but the other pirates stepped backwards to let their captain have the honour of opening it. The lid was carved with strange symbols. Chris lifted it slowly then gasped.

Piles of jewels, sapphires, rubies and diamonds glittered from the bottom of the chest. The pirates cheered again.

'Let's get this to our ship before the monster gets back,' Chris suggested.

'Aye aye, captain!' the pirates replied.

The four crew members grabbed a corner of the chest each and Chris led them down to the beach. All the while, he held out his cutlass menacingly to warn off any monsters.

THE PARTY

With the treasure safely stowed aboard the ship, they were off. The ship sailed smoothly over the crystal-clear water. The sky was a beautiful blue and the sun shone happily above the pirate crew.

When they docked the ship at the harbour, the pirate crew had a party. Chris was now Captain Moody and he was the happiest he had ever been. They all ate until their bellies burst and drank until they were drowning. It was a pirate's dream brought to life!

26
Modelled sentences

Simple statements

★ Chris was a fisherman.
★ He caught a bottle with his fishing rod.
★ Inside was a treasure map.
★ Chris rowed to shore.
★ He wanted to look like a pirate.
★ He bought a jacket, hat, sword and gun.
★ A crew of pirates needed a new captain.
★ Chris said he should be their captain.
★ Chris introduced himself as 'Captain Moody.'
★ He showed the pirate crew the treasure map.
★ The pirates agreed to be Chris's crew.
★ They made a new flag for their quest.
★ The pirates battled their way through the stormy seas.
★ They arrived at the treasure island.
★ They dropped the anchor.
★ They walked over the beach to the Forest of Doom.
★ There were bones everywhere inside the forest.
★ The pirates became scared.
★ They decided to leave.
★ The pirates sailed the boat to the top of the island.
★ They went straight to the Cave of Monsters to find the treasure.
★ They met a monster.
★ The crew ran away.
★ Chris had to fight the monster alone.
★ Chris hit the monster's claw with his cutlass.
★ It ran off.

* Chris and the pirates found the treasure inside the cave.
* They took the treasure to their ship.
* They sailed away.
* Chris and the pirates arrived home.
* They had a party.

B. QUESTIONS, EXCLAMATIONS AND COMMANDS

Questions

* Where would he find a crew**?**
* Where would he find a ship**?**
* 'What's your name then**?**' one pirate asked.
* What makes you think we'd be your crew**?**'
* 'What**?**' cried the crew, clearly appalled.
* 'What's wrong**?**' asked Chris.
* 'Erm, pirate crew**?**'

Exclamations

* It was so boring**!**
* 'Ooof**!**'
* He decided right then and there to become not a knight or a superhero or a dragon trainer but instead a … pirate**!**
* 'Yar**!**' he said, as he thought that was what a pirate might have said.
* Crew**!**
* 'Pirates**!**' Chris gasped.
* 'Your clothes look brand new**!**'
* 'Because I have this**!**'
* 'We're your crew**!**' they chorused together.
* 'That's the pirate way**!**' shouted Tina Tailor.
* 'It's dead**!**' grinned Peg Leg Pete.
* 'Aye aye, captain**!**' the pirates replied.

Commands

* '**Throw** him in the sea!' another bellowed, '**Feed** him to the sharks!'
* '**Get** rid of him!'
* '**Make** it as red as blood.'
* '**Cover** it in piratey things like skulls and swords.'
* '**Gather** around, crew,' Chris commanded.
* '**Park** there at the top.'
* '**Don't** go straight to the X either!' snarled Peg Leg Pete.
* '**Go** to each place first!' barked Mad Mary.
* '**Get** the treasure then,' smiled Mad Mary.

C. DESCRIPTION: EXPANDED NOUN PHRASES, SIMILES, ADVERBS, PREPOSITION PHRASES, DIALOGUE AND ALLITERATION

Expanded noun phrases

★ One day, Chris rowed his boat over the **calm and still sea**.

★ The fishing line was probably caught on a **jagged rock**.

★ The bottle was **old and dirty with a wooden stopper** in the top.

★ It had a **familiar black flag with a skull and crossed bones**.

★ They had a **red flag with a golden skull, white sword and blue hourglass timer**.

★ **Rainbow coloured fish** darted between **red, leafy coral**.

★ The pirates dropped anchor to the south of the **small tropical island**.

★ The **golden sandy beach** had **powdery sand**.

★ Gone were the **tropical waters, sandy beach and blazing sunshine**.

★ Stinky Sid rowed over a **stunning, rainbow coloured coral reef**.

★ The **grey tip of a shark's fin** sliced through the water.

★ **Huge, jagged rocks** guarded the island.

★ The **bleached bones of an enormous creature** blocked the mouth of the cave.

★ It brought Chris close to its **snapping jaws** that dripped saliva onto the rocks below.

★ There was a **huge wooden treasure chest** at the back of the cave.

★ They sailed over the **crystal-clear water**.

Similes

★ I want the flag to be **as red as blood**.

★ Clouds gathered above **like a flock of black sheep**.

★ He passed palm trees with huge leaves **like a fan**.

Adverbs

★ He stood up **quickly**.

★ He swam **wildly** away from the ship and the other pirates.

★ Chris pulled the treasure map **dramatically** from his belt.

★ 'No,' Chris said **firmly**.

★ The ship sailed **slowly** into the shallow reef.

★ The weather changed **instantly**.

★ The trees shook **slightly**.

★ High rocks rose **vertically** out of the sea.

★ 'Maybe this is the monster,' Stinky Sid said, **uncertainly**.

★ **Suddenly**, the monster roared again.

★ Saliva dripped **noisily** onto the rocks below.

★ The monster howled **loudly**.

★ It scuttled **rapidly** into the water.

★ The crew applauded **madly**.

★ Chris held out his cutlass **menacingly** to warn off any monsters.

* They sailed **smoothly** over the crystal-clear water.
* The sun shone **happily** above the pirate crew.

Preposition phrases

* He rowed in his little boat **across the sea**.
* It was caught **on a jagged rock**.
* **On the end of his hook** was a bottle.
* He tied his boat **to the pier**.
* He walked slowly **towards the ship**.
* The wind became a howling monster that lashed **at them from all around**.
* The ship sailed slowly **into a shallow reef**.
* Rainbow-coloured fish darted **between the red, leafy coral**.
* They dropped the anchor **to the south of the small tropical island**.
* A cold wind swept **through the forest**.
* White human and animal bones were scattered all **around the forest**.
* A stunning, rainbow coloured coral reef lay **beneath the surface of the water**.
* High rocks rose vertically **out of the sea**.
* The grey tip of a shark's fin sliced **through the water** nearby.
* Its snapping jaws dripped saliva noisily **onto the rocks below**.
* Jewels, sapphires, rubies and diamonds glittered **from the bottom of the chest**.
* The ship sailed smoothly **over the crystal-clear water**.
* They docked the ship **at the harbour**.

Dialogue

* **'What's your name then?'** one pirate asked.
* **'My name is Christopher Moody, but you can call me *Captain Moody*!'**
* **'Your clothes look brand new!'** another commented, **'What ships have you sailed on?'**
* **'Erm … the Good Ship Betty … Yar!'**
* **'Never heard of it,'** a third laughed, **'What makes you think we'd be your crew?'**
* **'Because I have this!'**
* **'What be your names … Yar!'**
* **'I'm Stinky Sid,'** one pirate replied.
* **'I'm Peg Leg Pete,'** another answered.
* **'I'm Mad Mary,'** a third cried.
* **'I'm Tina Tailor and I'll make us a new flag!'**
* **'Yeah, a better one than last time,'** Stinky Sid said, **'Let's put stuff like unicorns, butterflies and kittens on this time.'**
* **'Let's park there at the top!'** declared Chris, pointing at the Cave of Monsters with the red X.
* **'What?'** cried the crew, clearly appalled.

★ **'What's wrong?'** asked Chris.
★ **'You don't *park* a ship,'** growled Stinky Sid.
★ **'You don't go straight to the X either!'** snarled Peg Leg Pete.
★ **'You have to go to each place first!'** barked Mad Mary.
★ **'That's the pirate way!'** shouted Tina Tailor.
★ Chris shrugged and thought it best to just say, **'Yar!'**

Alliteration

★ **S**tinky **S**id
★ **P**eg Leg **P**ete
★ **M**ad **M**ary
★ **T**ina **T**ailor
★ **r**ocks **r**ose
★ **s**ailed **s**moothly

27
Innovating sentences model

STATEMENTS			
Chris	**was**	**a**	**fisherman.**
Chris	was	a	.
He	**wanted to be**	**a**	**pirate.**
He	wanted to be	a	.
He	**found**	**a**	**bottle.**
He	found	a	.
They	**arrived at**	**the**	**treasure island.**
They	arrived at	the	.
They	**met**	**a**	**monster.**
They	met	a	.
They found	**the treasure**		**inside the cave.**
They found			.
QUESTIONS			
Where would he find	**a**		**ship and crew?**
Where would he find	a		?
COMMANDS					
Go to	**the**	**Forest**	**of**	**Doom.**
Go to	the			.

EXPANDED NOUN PHRASES

It was	**old and**	**dirty**	**with a wooden stopper.**	
It was			with	
Huge	**jagged**	**rocks**	**guarded**	**the island.**
			guarded	the island.
They	**found a**	**huge**	**wooden**	**treasure chest.**
They	found a			.

SIMILES

The flag	**was**	**as red as blood.**
The flag	was	.

ADVERBS

He	**stood up**	**quickly.**	
He	stood up		.
Saliva	**dripped**	**noisily**	**onto the rocks.**
Saliva	dripped		onto the rocks.

PREPOSITIONS

He	**walked slowly**	**towards the ship.**
He	walked slowly	.
Bones	**were scattered**	**around the forest.**
	were scattered	.
Jewels	**glittered**	**from the bottom of the chest.**
	glittered	.

28
Coordination and subordination

Clause (1)	Conjunction	Clause (2)	√
Chris had always longed for adventure	**and**	a. he wanted to be a superhero.	
		b. he dreamed of being a knight.	
He was a fisherman	**and**	a. he had a little boat.	
		b. he found it boring.	
The flag was red	**and**	a. flapped in the wind.	
		b. had a golden skull on it.	
The Forest of Doom was scary	**so**	a. the pirates went straight to the X.	
		b. they followed Stinky Sid to the boat.	
The pirates got the treasure	**so**	a. they had a party.	
		b. Captain Moody was happy.	
Captain Moody had a cutlass	**so**	a. he could fight the monster.	
		b. that he could look like a real pirate.	
The pirates needed a new captain	**because**	a. they threw the other one into the sea.	
		b. they hadn't found any treasure in a long time.	
The monster was scary	**because**	a. it had the head of a shark.	
		b. of its terrible roar.	

Captain Moody was brave	because	a. he fought the monster.	
		b. he didn't run away like the others.	
Stinky Sid wanted unicorns on the flag	but	a. the other pirates wouldn't let him.	
		b. Chris told him he couldn't.	
The monster was huge	but	a. it was cowardly.	
		b. could still move quickly.	
The island was not far away	but	a. a storm made the journey difficult.	
		b. was a very different place.	
Chris gulped probably	because	a. he was scared.	
		b. he had never done this before.	
The pirates said, 'Yar!'	and	a. it was not the first time.	
		b. nodded in agreement.	
The monster ran away	because	a. he was frightened.	
		b. he had a sore claw.	

EXERCISE 1: COMBINING THE PHRASES INTO SENTENCES AND INTO A PARAGRAPH

Using *and, but, because* and *so* to develop sentence structure.
Complete the following sentence stems:

Chris had always longed for adventure **and**_____

He was a fisherman **and**_____

The flag was red **and**_____

The Forest of Doom was scary, **so**_____

The pirates found the treasure, **so**_____

Captain Moody had a cutlass **so**_____

The pirates needed a new captain **because**_____

The monster was scary **because**_____

Captain Moody was brave **because**_____

Stinky Sid wanted unicorns on the flag **but**_____

The monster was huge **but**_____

The island was not far away **but**_____

Chris gulped probably **because**_____

The pirates said, "Yar!" **and**_____

The monster ran away **because** _____

Examples

Chris had always longed for adventure **and** he wanted to be a superhero.

He was a fisherman **and** he found it boring.

The flag was red **and** flapped in the wind.

The Forest of Doom was scary, **so** they followed Stinky Sid to the boat.

The pirates found the treasure, **so** they had a party.

Captain Moody had a cutlass **so** that he could look like a real pirate.

The pirates needed a new captain **because** they threw the other one into the sea.

The monster was scary **because** of its terrible roar.

Captain Moody was brave **because** he fought the monster.

Stinky Sid wanted unicorns on the flag, **but** Chris told him he couldn't.

The monster was huge, **but** it was cowardly.

The island was not far away **but** was a very different place.

Chris gulped, probably **because** he was scared.

The pirates said, "Yar!" and nodded in agreement.

The monster ran away **because** it was frightened.

29
'Ruby Red'

My name is Ruby Red and I live in *'once upon a time'* in a village on the edge of a forest. You've probably heard of my cousin, Little Red Riding Hood. She was the one who got into a bit of bother with a wolf.

Like Little Red Riding Hood, or RRH for short, I also wear red, but then so do my father, mother, brother, uncle and aunt. Granny got a huge discount on a large roll of red cloth and has been making us all revolting red clothes for the past year. I really hate red! I look like a rotten radish.

Anyway, back to my story. Like RRH I also go to visit Granny and walk through the forest to take her a scrumptious picnic basket of home-made goodies. And like RRH, I once met a wolf. Luckily, it didn't eat me all up. But I must tell you, my story ended very, very differently from my cousin's.

THE FOREST

The day it happened was a sunny day and the forest was covered in beautiful bright sunlight. It had been raining for days, so I was glad to get out of the house. Mother had given me the usual warnings, 'Don't talk to strangers. Go straight to Granny's and don't wander off the path. Watch out for any wolves.' I intended to keep my promise, but as often happens I soon forgot.

I set off following the narrow, twisting path through the forest. I took deep breaths of the wonderful, fragrant scents of summer drifting through the air. Above me, in the treetops the birds were singing. Everywhere I looked there was a rainbow of bright colours. Petals like pink confetti were scattered over the ground. Enormous groups of red, purple and white blossoms hung from the branches. Vivid, lime green vines wound around the huge tree trunks.

I hadn't walked far when I spotted a clearing full of dazzling purple and white flowers like a carpet of glittering jewels. Granny loves flowers, so I decided to pick her a bunch. Somewhere in the back of my mind I seemed to remember my mother telling me not to pick wildflowers, but these flowers didn't look very wild. So, I set off through the forest towards the clearing.

As I walked through the forest, I could hear the leaves rustling all around me. I stopped for a moment and sat on a log to watch the birds. I listened to the cheerful chattering of the magpies and saw them busily fluttering from tree to tree to hide their stolen treasure.

I hadn't intended to stay long, but I was fascinated by the squirrels. Up and down, up and down they scampered and then sat on a branch to nibble at the nuts clutched between their tiny fingers.

I don't know how long I had been sitting on the log, but my tummy started to rumble. I must have missed my lunch! I was tempted to have a nibble of the loaf of bread in my picnic basket, but Mum would be really furious if she found out. 'Time to get moving,' I thought. I set off back to the path, but out of the corner of my eye I spotted clusters of bright berries hanging from the bushes. I could hear my mother's warning, 'Do not eat anything in the forest because it might be poisonous and make you extremely sick.' But I was really, really hungry, and the berries looked scrumptious. 'I'll try one. One can't make me sick,' I thought. So, off I went.

I picked the biggest, plumpest, brightest berry you have ever seen and popped it into my mouth. Immediately, a yummy sweet syrup exploded in my mouth and trickled down my fingers and chin. They were the sweetest, juiciest berries I had ever tasted, so I picked another and another until they had all gone. My fingers and face were stained with sticky red juice. 'Oh, no! Mum will definitely know I've been eating berries now,' I yelped. Quickly, I licked my sticky fingers and tried to scrub the juice off my face. My mum could get very, very cross. I should know. I've been in trouble often enough.

THE BERRIES

I had been so busy following the berry bushes, I hadn't noticed that I had walked deeper and deeper into the forest. Above my head, the trees were knotted together in a dark arch. Misty light shone through gaps in the trees and it made them look like ghostly statues. I was sure I had seen shadowy figures dancing wildly on the path in front of me.

I looked around nervously and tried to find something familiar to guide me back to the path. It was a total nightmare! I got terribly lost because I wandered around and around in circles. I ended up in a part of the forest I had never seen before. I was scratched and bruised. I couldn't see the tangled roots twisting and wriggling across the ground, and they kept tripping me up.

This part of the forest was deathly quiet, so every sound made me jump out of my skin. My heart was leaping like a salmon in my chest. I started to walk faster and faster, but I soon had to slow down because sharp thorns kept leaping out of the tangle of trees and bushes and grabbed at my coat and skirt.

I was sure I was being followed and kept looking over my shoulder. Suddenly, I heard the snap of a twig and froze. My eyes darted left and right as I tried to catch sight of any movement, but I couldn't see a thing. By now, not only was my heart thudding, there was also sweat streaming down my back. My hands were sweaty, and I kept having to rub them dry on my skirt.

My tummy had been making some very strange noises for a while and all of a sudden, a terrible pain tore through my stomach. I yelled in agony, bent over and clutched my stomach.

Wave after wave of agony rose through my body and I felt really sick. I tried to keep on walking, but it was no good. Finally, I gave up and slumped onto my knees. I wrapped my arms tightly around my middle and groaned and groaned and groaned.

Soon, the pain was unbearable and when I tried to stand up my head began to swim. I shouted, 'Help me, somebody! Is there anybody there? Help!' I waited and waited, and screamed and screamed until my throat was sore, but no one came.

Suddenly, I started to heave and retch. And then, bright red berry juice erupted in a frothy fountain from my mouth. Sweat poured down my forehead into my eyes, but I didn't have time to wipe it away. A wave of horrific pain like a clenched fist punched me in the stomach. When I retched, another stream of berry juice exploded from my mouth. I was sweating and shivering at the same time. My head was on fire.

Whenever I tried to stand up, my knees gave way and I ended up in a heap on the floor. I had to keep my eyes shut because every time I opened them the world spun madly round and round. Finally, the streams of berry juice vomit stopped, and I lay down and curled into a ball.

THE WOLF

I drifted in and out of sleep. I had a strange feeling that something or someone kept trying to wake me up. I thought I'd felt a warm breath on my cheek, but I couldn't open my eyes to look. Then, I felt something wiry tickle my face. Next, a nibble on my arm. Finally, I was jolted fully awake by a wet nuzzling on my fingers. I forced one eye open and glanced to the right. Standing over me was a wolf.

'Dragon's dung! I really should have listened to my mother,' I moaned. By now, I was resigned to my fate. I had no energy to run. I closed my eyes again and rolled over.

'Yes, dear girl. You should have listened to your mother. Never eat anything from the forest,' a deep voice boomed.

'Oh, help! Now I'm dreaming a wolf is talking to me,' I wailed and pressed my hands over my ears.

'Ouch!' I yelped. The wolf had nipped my hand.

'Come on. Get up. If you lie there much longer you will die from the poison and the cold.'

Slowly, I raised myself up onto my elbows. The wolf was sitting beside me and instead of snarling fangs I was looking into a pair of gentle amber eyes.

'Little girl, I am not going to eat you. Not all wolves try to eat little girls you know. I came because I knew you were in trouble.'

'I don't understand,' I said, puzzled. 'A wolf ate my Granny and tried to eat my cousin.'

'That would be my uncle. He was the wicked wolf of the family. He was the one who went around blowing down little pigs' houses, eating grannies and dressing up in their clothes. Because of him wolves have an awfully bad name. We're not safe anywhere now.'

'But isn't he dead?' I asked.

'Thankfully, yes! A terrible end really. First, he was boiled in a pot by the pigs and left with terrible burns all over his body. And that's why he stole your granny's clothes – to hide the scars. Finally, he lost his head to a woodcutter. And that was the end of him.'

'I'll tell everyone you saved my life and then we'll be friends,' I said excitedly.

'They'll never believe you. If you tell them you met me, we will be driven out of the forest again. They'll never understand that wolves only attack humans if we are threatened. We have never EVER eaten humans. We're partial to a chicken, the odd rabbit and a fish, but human flesh is tough and chewy like leather, so I've heard.' I was sure I heard the wolf chuckle.

'They will listen to me, I promise,' I begged.

'No! Swear to me that you will never tell anyone of our meeting,' he growled.

'I promise,' I said, but I did have my fingers crossed behind my back. That's why I can share this story with you.

Suddenly, I saw the wolf's nose twitch and his ears flick forward. He sniffed the air and his body tensed.

'It's time to get you back to your parents, Ruby. They are looking for you. I can hear them shouting your name.'

I hadn't heard anything, but I know wolves can hear things miles away.

The wolf crouched down. I clambered up onto his warm, grey back and held on tightly to his fur. He rose under me and shot off through the trees, threading his way between the tree trunks and leaping over fallen logs. Soon, we were back at the path and I could now hear my father's voice calling my name.

The wolf crouched down again and lowered me to the ground. 'This is where I leave you. Remember your promise, Ruby. Never tell anyone that we met.' He turned and raced back towards the trees.

He had just disappeared into the shadows when I saw my mother and father racing towards me. There was a lot of crying and hugging and my father carried me home. Later, there was a lot of scolding, a few punishments and some really disgusting medicine like bitter, black liquorice syrup.

In the past, I may not have kept my promises, but I now try very hard not to break a promise. I will never again eat anything from the forest unless it is given to me by a grown-up. I often wonder if the wolf would have become my friend if I'd kept my promise and not told anyone that I had met him in the forest. Every time I walk through the forest, I look for the wolf. Sometimes, I think I catch a brief glimpse of him, but since that day we have never met again.

30
Modelled sentences

A. STORY PLOT

Simple statements

- ★ My name is Ruby Red.
- ★ I live in *'once upon a time'* in a village by the forest.
- ★ Little Red Riding Hood is my cousin.
- ★ I wear red clothes.
- ★ I walk through the woods to visit Granny.
- ★ I take her a picnic basket.
- ★ I met a wolf.
- ★ The wolf rescued me.

Questions

- ★ 'Did the wolf eat me**?**' you ask.

Exclamations

- ★ I hate the colour red**!**

Commands

- ★ **Get** on with the story.

Expanded noun phrases

- ★ Granny got **a huge discount** on **a roll of bright red cloth**.
- ★ She has been making us **revolting red clothes**.
- ★ I take Granny a **scrumptious picnic basket of home-made goodies**.

Similes

★ I look **like a rotten radish**.

Adverbs

★ **Luckily**, it didn't eat me all up.

Prepositions

★ My village is **on the edge of the forest**.
★ I walk **through the forest** to take her a scrumptious picnic basket.

Alliteration

★ **R**uby **R**ed
★ **r**evolting **r**ed **c**lothes
★ **r**otten **r**adish

2. THE FOREST

STORY PLOT

Simple statements

★ It was a lovely sunny day.
★ I was glad to get out of the house.
★ Mother told me not to wander off the path.
★ I followed the path.
★ There were enormous red, purple and white flowers.
★ Granny loves flowers.
★ I decided to pick her a bunch.
★ I wandered off the path.
★ I listened to the birds singing.
★ I could see the squirrels scampering up the trees.
★ I was hungry.
★ I saw huge plump berries.
★ I ate all the juicy berries.

Questions

★ 'Will eating just one berry make me sick**?**' I wondered.

Exclamations

★ Oh no**!** I'm in big trouble.

Commands

- ★ **Do not** eat anything in the forest.
- ★ **Don't** talk to strangers. **Go** straight to Granny's.
- ★ **Don't** wander off the path.
- ★ **Watch** out for wolves.

Expanded noun phrases

- ★ I followed **the narrow, twisting path**.
- ★ I breathed in **the wonderful, fragrant scents of summer**.
- ★ **Enormous groups of red, purple and white blossoms** hung from the branches.
- ★ **Vivid, lime green vines** wound around the **huge tree trunks**.
- ★ I spotted a clearing full of **dazzling purple and white flowers**.
- ★ I listened to the **cheerful chattering of the magpies**.
- ★ The squirrels clutched the nuts between their **tiny fingers**.
- ★ I saw **clusters of bright berries** hanging from the bushes.
- ★ **The plump, ripe, juicy berries** were scrumptious.
- ★ **A yummy sweet syrup** exploded in my mouth.
- ★ My face was stained with **sticky red juice**.

Similes

- ★ **Petals like pink confetti** were scattered over the ground.
- ★ The clearing was covered in purple and white **flowers like a carpet of dazzling jewels**.

Adverbs

- ★ I watched the magpies **busily** fluttering from tree to tree.
- ★ **Immediately**, a yummy sweet syrup exploded in my mouth.
- ★ I **quickly** licked my sticky fingers and tried to scrub the juice off my face.

Prepositions

- ★ I was glad to get **out of the house**.
- ★ Wonderful, fragrant scents of summer drifted **through the air**.
- ★ The birds were singing **in the treetops above my head**.
- ★ Beautiful red, purple, yellow and white flowers hung **from the branches**.
- ★ Vivid green vines wound **around the huge tree trunks**.
- ★ I sat **on a log** to watch the magpies.
- ★ The squirrels scampered **up and down the tree trunks**.
- ★ They sat **on a branch** to nibble their nuts.
- ★ **Out of the corner of my eye**, I spotted lots of delicious bright berries.
- ★ I popped the berry **into my mouth**.
- ★ I tried to scrub the sticky juice **off my face**.

Alliteration

- ★ **b**eautiful **b**right sunlight
- ★ **s**ummer **s**cents
- ★ **ch**eerful **ch**attering of the magpies
- ★ **b**ig, **b**right berries
- ★ **st**icky **s**weet **s**yrup

Dialogue

- ★ '**Time to get moving**,' I said.
- ★ I could hear my mother's warning, '**Do not eat anything in the forest**.'
- ★ '**I'll try one. One can't make me sick**,' I thought.
- ★ '**Oh no! Mum will definitely know I've been eating berries now**,' I yelped.

3. THE BERRIES

STORY PLOT

Simple statements

- ★ I had walked deeper and deeper into the forest.
- ★ I looked around nervously.
- ★ I got terribly lost.
- ★ I was scratched and bruised.
- ★ It was deathly quiet.
- ★ I walked faster and faster.
- ★ I was sure I was being followed.
- ★ There was a terrible pain in my stomach.
- ★ I yelled in agony.
- ★ I couldn't walk.
- ★ I shouted for someone to help me.
- ★ No one came.
- ★ I was very sick.
- ★ I lay down and dozed off.

Questions

- ★ Is there anybody there**?**

Exclamations

- ★ Help me**!**
- ★ It was a total nightmare**!**

Commands

- ★ **Don't** lie down.

Expanded noun phrases

- ★ The trees were knotted together in a **dark arch**.
- ★ **Misty light** shone through gaps in the trees.
- ★ I had seen **shadowy figures** dancing on the path.
- ★ I couldn't see the **tangled, twisted roots** across the ground. It was **deathly quiet**.
- ★ **Sharp, prickly thorns** leapt out of the tangle of trees and bushes.
- ★ **A terrible pain** tore through my stomach.
- ★ **Wave after wave of agony** rose through my body.
- ★ **Bright red berry juice** erupted in **a frothy stream** from my mouth.

Similes

- ★ The misty light made the **trees look like ghostly statues**.
- ★ My heart was **leaping like a salmon in my chest**.
- ★ I had a pain **like a clenched fist punching me in the stomach**.

Adverbs

- ★ I had seen shadowy figures dancing **wildly** on the path.
- ★ I looked around **nervously**.
- ★ **Suddenly**, I heard the snap of a twig.
- ★ **Finally**, I gave up and slumped onto my knees.
- ★ I wrapped my arms **tightly** around my middle.
- ★ The world spun **madly** round and round when I opened my eyes.
- ★ The streams of berry juice vomit stopped **finally**.

Prepositions

- ★ I had walked deeper **into the forest**.
- ★ **Above my head**, the trees were knotted together in a dark arch.
- ★ Misty light shone **through gaps in the trees**.
- ★ Shadowy figures danced **on the path in front of me**.
- ★ Tangled roots wriggled **across the ground**.
- ★ Every sound made me jump **out of my skin**.
- ★ Sharp thorns leapt **out of the tangle of trees and bushes**.
- ★ I kept looking **over my shoulder**.
- ★ Sweat streamed **down my back**.
- ★ I rubbed my hands dry **on my skirt**.
- ★ I slumped **onto my knees**.
- ★ I wrapped my arms **around my middle**.

* The pain was **like a clenched fist punching me in the stomach**.
* Red juice erupted **from my mouth**.
* I ended up in a heap **on the floor**.

Alliteration

* **b**erry **b**ushes
* **s**weat **s**treaming
* **f**rothy **f**ountain

Dialogue

* **'Help me!'** I yelled.
* I shouted, **'Is there anybody there?'**

4. THE WOLF

STORY PLOT

Simple statements

* I drifted in and out of sleep.
* I thought someone was trying to wake me up.
* I felt a warm breath on my cheek.
* I was jolted awake.
* The wolf was standing over me.
* He told me to get up.
* He told me the bad wolf was his uncle.
* His uncle had tried to eat Red Riding Hood and Granny.
* Wolves like chicken, rabbit and fish.
* Wolves don't like human flesh.
* He made me promise not to tell anyone I had met him.
* The wolf heard my parents shouting for me.
* He carried me on his back to the path.
* He disappeared into the forest.
* My parents were very happy to see me.
* I was in a lot of trouble.
* I never saw the wolf again.

Questions

* But isn't he dead**?**

Exclamations

* Dragons' Dung**!**
* Oh, help**!**

- ★ Ouch**!**
- ★ No**!**

Commands

- ★ **Get** up.
- ★ **Swear** to me that you will never tell anyone of our meeting.

Expanded noun phrases

- ★ I had a **strange feeling** someone was trying to wake me up.
- ★ I felt a **warm breath** on my cheek.
- ★ There was a **wet nuzzling** on my fingers.
- ★ I looked into a **pair of gentle amber eyes**.
- ★ He was left with **terrible burns** all over his body.
- ★ I climbed onto his **warm, grey back**.
- ★ He leapt over **fallen logs**.
- ★ I had to take **disgusting medicine**.

Similes

- ★ Human flesh is **tough and chewy like leather**.
- ★ I had to take disgusting **medicine like bitter, black liquorice syrup**.

Adverbs

- ★ **Then**, I felt something wiry tickle my face.
- ★ **Next**, there was a nibble on my arm.
- ★ **Slowly**, I raised myself up onto my elbows.
- ★ **First**, he was boiled in a pot by the pigs.
- ★ **Finally**, he lost his head to a woodcutter.
- ★ 'I tell everyone you saved my life and then we'll be friends,' I said **excitedly**.
- ★ **Suddenly**, I saw the wolf's nose twitch.
- ★ I held on **tightly** to his fur.
- ★ **Sometimes**, I think I catch a brief glimpse of the wolf.

Prepositions

- ★ I felt a warm breath **on my cheek**.
- ★ Something nibbled **on my arm**.
- ★ I glanced **to the right**.
- ★ Standing **over me** was a wolf.
- ★ I pressed my hands **over my ears**.
- ★ The wolf was sitting **beside me**.
- ★ I looked **into a pair of gentle amber eyes**.
- ★ He was boiled **in a pot** and had terrible burns all **over his body**.

★ I crossed my fingers **behind my back**.
★ I climbed up **onto his warm, grey back**.
★ He threaded his way **between the tree trunks** and leaped **over fallen logs**.
★ He disappeared **into the shadows**.

ALLITERATION

★ **D**ragons' **D**ung
★ **w**icked **w**olf
★ **b**lack, **b**itter liquorice syrup

DIALOGUE

★ **'Dragon's Dung! I really should have listened to my mother**,' I moaned.
★ **'Yes, dear girl. You should have listened to your mother**,' a deep voice boomed.
★ **'Now I'm dreaming a wolf is talking to me**,' I wailed, pressing my hands over my ears.
★ **'Ouch!'** I yelped.
★ **'I don't understand**,' I said, puzzled.
★ **'But isn't he dead?'** I asked.
★ **'I'll tell everyone you saved my life and then we'll be friends**,' I said excitedly.
★ **'We're partial to a chicken, the odd rabbit and a fish, but human flesh is tough and chewy like leather, so I've heard**.' The wolf chuckled.
★ **'They will listen to me, I promise**,' I begged.
★ **'No! Swear to me that you will never tell anyone of our meeting**,' he growled.
★ **'I promise**,' I said, crossing my fingers behind my back.
★ **'Remember your promise, Ruby. Never tell anyone that we met**,' the wolf warned and raced back towards the trees.

31
Innovating sentences model

STATEMENTS					
It	**was**	**a**	**lovely**	**sunny**	**day**.
It	was	a			day.
Mother	**told me**	**not**	**to wander off the path.**		
Mother	told me	not	to .		
I	**followed**	**the**	**narrow**	**path**.	
I	followed	the			.
There were	**enormous**	**red, purple and white**		**flowers.**	
There were				flowers.	
There were	enormous				.

STATEMENTS:				
I	**could hear**	**the**	**birds**	**singing.**
I	could hear	the		.
I	**could see**	**the**	**squirrels**	**scampering up the trees.**
I	could see	the		.

I	ate	all the	juicy	berries.
I	ate	all the		.

QUESTIONS					
Will	**eating**	**one**	**berry**	**make me**	**sick?**
Will	eating	one		make me	sick?
Will	eating	one		make me	?
EXCLAMATIONS:					
Oh no!	**I'm in**		**big**	**trouble.**	
	I'm in			.	

COMMANDS:			
Do not	**eat**	**anything**	**in the forest.**
Do not		anything	.
Don't	**talk**	**to**	**strangers.**
Don't	talk	to	.
Don't	**wander**	**off**	**the path.**
Don't	wander		.
Watch out	**for**	**wolves.**	
Watch out	for		.

EXPANDED NOUN PHRASES						
I	followed	the	narrow	twisting		path.
I	followed	the				path.
Enormous	**groups of**	**red**	**purple**	**white**	**blossoms**	**hung from the branches.**
Enormous	groups of				blossoms	hung from the branches.

I	spotted	clusters	of		bright	berries.		
I	spotted	clusters	of					.
The	plump	ripe	juicy		berries	were	scrumptious.	
The			juicy			were		.
A	yummy	sweet	syrup	exploded		in my mouth.		
A				exploded		in my mouth.		
My	face	was	stained	with	sticky	red		juice.
My		was	stained	with				juice.

SIMILES				
Petals	like pink confetti		were scattered over the ground.	
Petals	like		were scattered over the ground.	
The	clearing	was covered in	flowers	like a carpet of dazzling jewels.
The	clearing	was covered in	flowers	like .

ADVERBS						
I	watched	the	magpies	fluttering	busily	from tree to tree.
I	watched	the	magpies			from tree to tree.
I	watched	the				from tree to tree.
Immediately	a	yummy	sweet	syrup	exploded	in my mouth.
	a	yummy	sweet	syrup		in my mouth.
	a				exploded	in my mouth.

ADVERBS:					
I	quickly	licked	my	sticky	fingers.
I		licked	my		fingers.
I			my		.

PREPOSITIONS					
I	**was**	**glad**	**to**	**get**	**out of the house.**
I	was	glad	to		.

Birds	**were singing**		**in the treetops**	**above my head.**
Birds	were singing			.

Vivid	**green**	**vines**	**wound**	**around the tree trunks.**
Vivid	green	vines		.

I	**sat**	**on a log**	**to watch**	**the magpies.**
I			to watch	.

PREPOSITIONS:			
Out of the corner of my eye	**I**	**spotted**	**lots of delicious bright berries.**
Out of the corner of my eye	I	spotted	.

I tried to	**to**	**scrub**	**the sticky juice**	**off my face.**
I tried to	to	scrub	the sticky juice	.
I tried to	to	scrub		.

32
Coordination and subordination

Clause (1)	Conjunction	Clause (2)	√
My name is Ruby Red	**and**	a. I live *'once upon a time'*.	
		b. call me Ruby.	
I wear red clothes	**but**	a. I love red.	
		b. I really hate red.	
All my family wear red clothes	**because**	a. my granny had a large roll of red cotton.	
		b. blue is our favourite colour.	
I am here to tell you my story	**so**	a. I nearly didn't make it.	
		b. the wolf obviously didn't eat me.	

EXERCISE 1: COMBINING THE PHRASES INTO SENTENCES AND INTO A PARAGRAPH

Using *and, but, because* and *so* to develop sentence structure.
Complete the following sentence stems:

My name is Ruby Red **and** _____

I wear red clothes **but**_____

All my family wear red clothes **because** _____

I am here to tell you my story, **so** _____

Examples

My name is Ruby Red, **and** I live in *'once upon a time.'*
I wear red clothes, **but** I really hate red.
All my family wear red clothes **because** my granny had a large roll of red cotton.
I am here to tell you my story, **so** the wolf obviously didn't eat me.

2. THE BERRIES

Clause (1)	Conjunction	Clause (2)	√
It was a sunny day	**and**	a. the forest was covered in beautiful bright sunlight.	
		b. the path was very dark.	
It had been raining for days	**so**	a. it was very dry.	
		b. I was glad to get out of the house.	
I meant to keep my promise	**but**	a. my mother would get very cross.	
		b. I soon forgot.	
Granny loved flowers	**so**	a. I decided to pick her a bunch.	
		b. they made her sneeze.	
My mother told me not to pick wildflowers	**but**	a. I decided not to pick any.	
		b. these flowers didn't look very wild.	
I stopped for a moment	**and**	a. sat on a log to watch the birds.	
		b. skipped around the trees.	
I hadn't intended to stay long	**but**	a. I only watched for five minutes.	
		b. I was fascinated by the squirrels.	
They scampered up and down the trees	**and**	a. they were very tired.	
		b. then sat on a branch to nibble their nuts.	
I set off back to the path	**but**	a. I spotted clusters of bright, juicy berries.	
		b. I needed to get to Granny's house.	
I was really, really hungry	**and**	a. the berries looked revolting.	
		b. the berries looked scrumptious.	
I picked the biggest, plumpest, brightest berry	**and**	a. it dropped on the floor.	
		b. popped it into my mouth.	

They were the sweetest, juiciest berries I had ever tasted	**so**	a. I picked another and another.	
		b. I spat them out.	
I knew I had missed my lunch	**because**	a. my tummy was rumbling.	
		b. I had eaten the berries.	
I hadn't walked far	**when**	a. I picked another.	
		b. I spotted a clearing full of brightly coloured flowers.	

EXERCISE 1: COMBINING THE PHRASES INTO SENTENCES AND INTO A PARAGRAPH

Using *and*, *but*, *because* and *so* to develop sentence structure.
Complete the following sentence stems:

It was a sunny day **and** _____

It had been raining for days, **so** _____

I meant to keep my promise, **but** _____

Granny loved flowers, **so** _____

My mother told me not to pick wildflowers, **but** _____

I stopped for a moment **and** _____

I hadn't intended to stay long, **but** _____

The squirrels scampered up and down the trees **and** _____

I set off back to the path, **but** _____

I was really hungry **and** _____

I picked the biggest, plumpest, brightest berry **and** _____

They were the sweetest, juiciest berries I had ever tasted, **so** _____

I knew I had missed lunch **because** _____

I hadn't walked far **when** _____

Examples

It was a sunny day **and** the forest was covered in beautiful bright sunlight.

It had been raining for days, **so** I was glad to get out of the house.

I meant to keep my promise, **but** I soon forgot.

Granny loved flowers, **so** I decided to pick her a bunch.

My mother told me not to pick wildflowers, **but** these flowers didn't look very wild.

I stopped for a moment **and** sat on a log to watch the birds.

I hadn't intended to stay long, **but** I was fascinated by the squirrels.

The squirrels scampered up and down the trees **and** then sat on a branch to nibble their nuts.

I set off back to the path, **but** I spotted clusters of bright, juicy berries.

I was really, really hungry, **and** the berries looked scrumptious.

I picked the biggest, plumpest, brightest berry **and** popped it into my mouth.

They were the sweetest, juiciest berries I had ever tasted, **so** I picked another and another.

I knew I had missed lunch **because** my tummy was rumbling.

I hadn't walked far **when** I spotted a clearing full of brightly coloured flowers.

3. THE FOREST

Clause (1)	Conjunction	Clause (2)	√
Misty light shone through the trees	and	a. made them look like ghostly statues.	
		b. I couldn't see anything.	
I looked around nervously	and	a. I was lost.	
		b. tried to find the way back to the main path.	
Tangled roots wriggled across the ground	and	a. leapt out of the bushes.	
		b. tripped me up.	
The forest was deathly quiet	so	a. every sound made me jump out of my skin.	
		b. it was dusk.	
Sharp thorns leapt out of the tangled bushes	and	a. grabbed my coat and skirt.	
		b. tickled my legs.	
I was sure I was being followed	and	a. kept looking over my shoulder.	
		b. kept hearing twigs snapping.	
I heard the snap of a twig	and	a. froze to the spot.	
		b. spun around.	
I watched for any movement	but	a. my head was spinning.	
		b. I couldn't see a thing.	
My hands were sweaty	so	a. I rubbed them dry on my skirt.	
		b. I was really scared.	

I yelled in agony	**and**	a. the pain was horrific.	
		b. clutched my stomach.	
I shouted for help	**but**	a. no-one came.	
		b. I could hear the woodcutter.	
The streams of berry juice vomit stopped	**and**	a. I lay on the ground.	
		b. I was very thirsty.	
I was terribly lost	**because**	a. I couldn't find the way to the path.	
		b. I had wandered around in circles.	
My head began to spin	**when**	a. I tried to get up.	
		b. I hopped on the spot.	
I screamed	**until**	a. I yelled for help.	
		b. my throat was sore.	

EXERCISE 1: COMBINING THE PHRASES INTO SENTENCES AND INTO A PARAGRAPH

Using *and*, *but*, *because* and *so* to develop sentence structure.
Complete the following sentence stems:

Misty light shone through the trees **and** _____

I looked around nervously **and** _____

Tangled roots wriggled across the ground **and**_____

The forest was deathly quiet, **so** _____

Sharp thorns leapt out of the tangled bushes **and** _____

I was sure I was being followed **and** _____

I heard the snap of a twig **and** _____

I watched for any movement, **but** _____

My hands were sweaty, **so** _____

I yelled in agony **and** _____

I shouted for help, **but** _____

The streams of berry juice vomit stopped **and** _____

I was terribly lost **because** _____

My head began to spin **when** _____

I screamed **until** _____

Examples

Misty light shone through the trees **and** made them look like ghostly statues.

I looked around nervously **and** tried to find the way back to the main path.

Tangled roots wriggled across the ground **and** tripped me up.

The forest was deathly quiet, **so** every sound made me jump out of my skin.

Sharp thorns leapt out of the tangled bushes **and** grabbed my coat and skirt.

I was sure I was being followed **and** kept looking over my shoulder.

I heard the snap of a twig **and** froze to the spot.

I watched for any movement, **but** I couldn't see a thing.

My hands were sweaty, **so** I rubbed them dry on my skirt.

I yelled in agony **and** clutched my stomach.

I shouted for help, **but** no one came.

The streams of berry juice vomit stopped, **and** I lay on the ground.

I was terribly lost **because** I had wandered around in circles.

My head began to spin **when** I tried to get up.

I screamed **until** my throat was sore.

4. THE WOLF

Clause (1)	Conjunction	Clause (2)	√
I felt a warm breath on my cheek	**but**	a. it tickled.	
		b. I couldn't open my eyes to see what it was.	
I forced one eye open	**and**	a. glanced to the right.	
		b. I felt excited.	
All wolves will be driven out of the forest	**so**	a. you must promise not to tell anyone.	
		b. humans are scared of us.	
My uncle had terrible burns	**so**	a. he was very embarrassed.	
		b. he stole your granny's clothes.	
The woodcutter chopped off his head	**and**	a. he is still stealing old lady's clothes.	
		b. that was the end of him.	

Wolves like chicken, rabbit and fish	**but**	a. do not eat humans.	
		b. we love human flesh.	
I promised I wouldn't tell anyone	**but**	a. I had my fingers crossed.	
		b. I was determined to keep my promise.	
I climbed onto the wolf's back	**and**	a. held on tightly.	
		b. shot off through the trees.	
The wolf rose under me	**and**	a. held on tightly.	
		b. shot off through the trees.	
He dodged around the tree trunks	**and**	a. leapt over fallen logs.	
		b. hit his head on the branch.	
The wolf crouched down	**and**	a. leapt over the ditch.	
		b. lowered me to the ground.	
My parents were very happy to see me	**but**	a. I was still in a lot of trouble.	
		b. I was not in any trouble.	
I think I have seen the wolf in the forest	**but**	a. we meet up every week.	
		b. we have never met again.	
I came	**because**	a. I knew you were in trouble.	
		b. I like children.	
Wolves have a really bad name	**because**	a. we are not nasty.	
		b. of the things my uncle did.	
He stole your granny's clothes	**because**	a. he was cold.	
		b. he wanted to hide the terrible scars all over his body.	
Wolves only attack humans	**when**	a. we are threatened.	
		b. we are hungry.	
I look for the wolf	**when**	a. I'm in bed.	
		b. I walk through the forest.	
Perhaps the wolf doesn't want to see me	**because**	a. I kept my promise.	
		b. I didn't keep my promise.	

EXERCISE 1: COMBINING THE PHRASES INTO SENTENCES AND INTO A PARAGRAPH

Using *and*, *but*, *because* and *so* to develop sentence structure.
Complete the following sentence stems:

I felt a warm breath on my cheek, **but** _____

I forced one eye open **and** _____

All wolves will be driven out of the forest, **so** _____

My uncle had terrible burns, **so** _____

The woodcutter chopped off his head, **and** _____

Wolves like chicken, rabbit and fish, **but** _____

I promised I wouldn't tell anyone, **but** _____

I climbed onto the wolf's back **and** _____

The wolf rose under me **and** _____

He dodged around the tree trunks **and** _____

The wolf crouched down **and** _____

My parents were very happy to see me, **but** _____

I came **because** _____

Wolves have a really bad name **because** _____

He stole your granny's clothes **because** _____

Wolves only attack humans **when** _____

I look for the wolf **when** _____

Perhaps the wolf doesn't want to see me **because** _____

Examples

I felt a warm breath on my cheek, **but** I couldn't open my eyes to see what it was.

I forced one eye open **and** glanced to the right.

All wolves will be driven out of the forest, **so** you must promise not to tell anyone.

My uncle had terrible burns, **so** he stole your granny's clothes.

The woodcutter chopped off his head, **and** that was the end of him.

Wolves like chicken, rabbit and fish, **but** do not eat human flesh.

I promised I wouldn't tell anyone, **but** I had my fingers crossed.

I climbed onto the wolf's back **and** held on tightly.

The wolf rose under me **and** shot off through the trees.

He dodged around the tree trunks **and** leapt over fallen logs.

The wolf crouched down **and** lowered me to the ground.

My parents were very happy to see me, **but** I was still in a lot of trouble.

I came **because** I knew you were in trouble.

Wolves have a really bad name **because** of the things my uncle did.

He stole your granny's clothes **because** he wanted to hide the terrible scars all over his body.

Wolves only attack humans **when** we are threatened.

I look for the wolf **when** I walk through the forest.

Perhaps the wolf doesn't want to see me **because** I didn't keep my promise.

33
'Jack and the Crystal Fang'

Long, long ago, a terrible plague spread throughout the land. In towns and villages, people locked themselves in their homes. Crops rotted in the fields. All work had stopped. Every village had the fever and sickness.

According to an ancient legend, the only cure was a powder made from the crystal fang of a dragon. This dragon was known to have its den in a cave in the north of the country and was known as *the Great Dragon of the North.*

King Arthur sent his knights to the north to search for the dragon's den. They had searched and searched far and wide, but no-one had ever found the entrance.

One day, Merlin, King Arthur's most famous wizard, returned from the mysterious valleys of South Wales. Merlin knew the location of the dragon's den, but he also knew that it could only be entered by a special boy born with a silver mark on his right hand.

Eight years before, Merlin had taken this boy, who was called Jack, to live with a family in a village in the North until the time came when his powers were needed. Over the years, Merlin had visited Jack often and had watched him grow into a caring, hard-working young boy.

As the plague had spread through the land, Merlin had visited Jack and told him of the quest that awaited him. He had instructed him that on the sixth day of the New Moon, Jack was to climb to the top of Dragon Ridge and Merlin would meet him there.

That is where our tale begins.

DRAGON RIDGE MOUNTAIN

It was early morning and the top of the mountain was lit by brilliant, golden sunshine. Jack squinted into the sun and looked for the path to the dragon's cave. He could see the icy summit and the jagged, deadly peaks like daggers. A bubbling stream tumbled down the mountain. He stared at the steep rocky slopes, but he could not see the entrance to the dragon's cave. It was hard to find the path because the bottom of the slope was covered in mist like a white fleecy blanket.

Jack's heart dropped. 'How am I going to find the path now?' he thought anxiously. 'How am I going to rescue the village?' Jack groaned and slumped against a boulder.

Suddenly, Jack heard a voice roar in his head. 'Use the beans.'

Jack had forgotten about the beans in his pouch. He didn't know how they could help, but he had no other plan. Jack put his hand in the pouch around his waist. The beans felt warm and hairy and a disgusting cheesy smell rose from the pouch. He quickly threw the beans on the ground.

Immediately, an odd tingling trickled through his body. When Jack looked up the mist had parted. Now, he could clearly see a narrow, winding path up the side of the mountain. The beans were magic!

He could see things far, far away. He could see the smallest rock and tiny creatures. Then, he spotted the entrance to the dragon's cave hidden behind three big, black boulders.

Jack closed his eyes. Instantly, he could see the inside of the cave. Enormous skeletons covered the floor of the cave. He could not see or hear the dragon, but he could smell smoke, burning flesh and rotten eggs.

When he opened his eyes, Jack's stomach lurched. 'Oh no!' he gasped. Huge, dark clouds raced towards the mountain. 'I can't turn back now,' thought Jack, gritting his teeth.

Somewhere above him, Jack heard Merlin shout, 'Get moving now.'

Jack knew there was no time to lose, so he started to climb.

THE STORM

Jack stepped onto the path and into a tunnel of swirling, cold mist. It was like a giant creature was sending its huge icy breaths down from the top of the mountain. The mist floated above his head, curled around his body and slithered over his feet.

Hour after hour, Jack trudged on and on. Slowly, he climbed and scrambled his way towards the icy summit. He crawled along narrow ledges and clambered over big black boulders like giant marbles scattered across the path. Finally, Jack thought he was getting closer to the top because he could feel the air getting colder.

Although Jack knew his climb was coming to an end, he was getting tired and his legs were aching. He didn't think he could climb much further, but the thought of his parents urged him on. 'Not far now. Keep going, Jack,' he kept muttering to himself.

But Jack's luck had run out. The storm had arrived: first, a rumble of thunder in the distance and then the whistle of the wind around the mountain. Before long, the thunder crashed and howled over his head. The wind whined and shrieked as it tore the mist into ragged sheets. Huge boiling black clouds raced towards the mountain.

The wind shoved and tugged fiercely at Jack and he struggled to stay on his feet. It made it impossible to walk. Jack was sure he would be blown off the path. 'Where are you, Merlin? Help me!' Jack yelled.

The thunder roared louder. Then, lightning like a flashing spear lit up the path. Next came the rain. It hammered on his back and stung his face. It was as if he was being blasted by a fire hose, and Jack was soaked from head to foot. It was hard to breathe. It was hard to walk, and Jack wasn't sure he would make it, but he kept on climbing.

Suddenly, a loud crack made Jack jump out of his skin. He looked up and froze. An enormous dazzling arrow of lightning lit up the sky. It ripped through the clouds and struck the path in front of him. Jack pressed his back against the side of the mountain and held his breath as a giant crack appeared at his feet. There was nowhere to go. He was trapped. 'Merlin. Help me!' Jack sobbed as the ledge disappeared and he tumbled through the air into the dark void below.

MERLIN

Jack spun wildly head over heels through the air. It felt as if his ears were going to burst. His eyes were bulging out of their sockets. Jack braced himself for the impact with the ground. But it never came.

One moment he was tumbling through the air towards the ground and the next Jack felt a fleecy pillow slide underneath him. When he opened his eyes, he saw that he was surrounded by what looked like a giant ball of cotton wool. All around him was brilliant white. He was in the middle of a cloud, and it was drifting slowly beneath him.

Suddenly, the movement stopped. The bottom of the cloud slid open like a trap door and deposited Jack on the ground. When he looked up, the cloud had vanished like a puff of smoke.

Jack looked around. He was at the entrance to the dragon's cave and Merlin was waiting for him.

'I thought I was too late.' Merlin's voice boomed out across the mountain.

'I d…d…didn't th…think I was g…g…going to make it,' Jack stammered. He could barely speak. His teeth were chattering and his whole body was shaking. The cold and damp from his sodden clothes had seeped into his bones and was making him shiver uncontrollably.

Jack squeezed out the sleeve of his wet tunic and looked up at Merlin towering above him. His long white hair and beard blew in the wind. Merlin really was a terrifying figure.

'You ch…ch…chose the wr…wrong b…b…b…boy, ssssir,' Jack stammered. 'I ammm nn… not b…b….brave. I… am n….n….not sss…str…strong. I…I…I am not cl…clever.'

Merlin leaned towards Jack and put an arm around his shoulder. He pointed at the silver mark on Jack's right hand. 'This is how I know, Jack that you are the boy the legends speak of.' Merlin raised his huge bronze staff and moved it slowly around Jack. A hot wind gusted around Jack's legs, then his body and finally his arms and head. Jack's clothes were soon dry.

'You need to get your strength back before you face the dragon,' Merlin said, guiding Jack towards a boulder and sitting down beside him. Merlin put his hand inside his long, woollen cloak and pulled out a wooden tankard. He handed it to Jack. The smell of cinnamon and honey wafted up Jack's nose. It was bubbling and it warmed his hands.

'Come on, down in one. You'll feel better once you have something warm inside you,' Merlin said kindly.

Slowly, Jack lifted the tankard to his dry lips and took a tiny sip. A delicious sweet taste flooded his mouth. Jack was very thirsty and drank it down in one gulp. Energy raced through his body like an electric current. 'Thank you, Merlin,' Jack said, handing the tankard back to the wizard.

'Do you feel better now?' Merlin asked. Jack nodded. 'Good. We haven't got long. We need to move fast. Listen carefully. The roast duck I left for the dragon has gone, so it should be asleep soon. But the sleeping potion I sprinkled on it is a new recipe and I'm not sure how long it will last.'

'Crows' claws! Do you mean the dragon might wake up while I'm trying to get its fang?' Jack said, his eyes wide with fear. 'I can't do this!' he said, shaking his head.

Merlin stared at him a moment and then pulled out a pink stone dangling from a leather thread. He leant over and hung it around Jack's neck. 'Wear this. It will protect and guide you. It is you, Jack, and you alone that can rid this land of the plague. In every family, every house, every village, there is sickness, fever and death. With the dragon fang you will create a kingdom free of disease and sickness. We are all relying on you, Jack.'

Jack took a deep breath. 'But what do I do if it discovers me before the sleeping potion works? How do I extract the crystal fang? What do I do if it wakes up?'

'So many questions,' Merlin chuckled. 'Never fear, Jack. I will be there to guide you.'

'If you are with me, I will try,' Jack said quietly.

Merlin nodded. 'When you enter the cave, you will see a tunnel ahead of you. Follow this tunnel until you come to a second cave where there is an enormous pit in the centre. But stay away from the pit. This is where you will find the dragon.' Merlin paused to make sure Jack understood his instructions.

Jack nodded.

'If the dragon finds you before the sleeping potion has worked, stand still and look it in the eye. Hold the crystal in your right hand. It will light up the mark on your hand. Whatever you do, do not look away.'

'What will happen if I look away?' Jack whispered.

'You will no longer be protected.' Merlin replied. Jack nodded. His heart was racing at the thought of staring into the eyes of a dragon.

Merlin dug inside his cloak and pulled out a leather bundle. Carefully, he unwrapped the leather parcel to reveal a purple paste. 'Wait until the dragon is asleep, then rub this paste onto its gums.'

Jack leant over to look at the paste, but quickly raised his head. It stunk of beetles, bats and bitter berries.

Merlin smiled. 'It doesn't smell good, but it will work. The fang will drop out quickly, so make sure you have your hands ready to catch it. Then wrap it carefully in the leather pouch.'

'Aren't you coming with me?" Jack asked.

'No, Jack. I cannot enter the cave, but that stone is my eyes and ears. I will be able to guide you through the stone and I will be waiting for you when you return.' Merlin closed the leather parcel and handed it to Jack, who slid it into the pouch around his waist.

Suddenly, Merlin stood up and beckoned for Jack to follow him. 'It's time, Jack.'

THE PORTAL

'Stand in front of the centre boulder,' Merlin told Jack.

Jack glanced to his right and watched as first Merlin grasped his golden staff in both hands and then raised it above his head. In a voice that echoed around the mountain, he said: 'Through the power of all that is good, I ask you to show this boy the way.'

Jack could not take his eyes off the bright light glowing from the end of the staff. A sudden gust of wind whirled around Merlin, sending his cloak flapping like giant wings around him.

When the wind had died down, Merlin lowered the staff onto the centre boulder. He closed his eyes and slowly rocked backwards and forwards. It was as if he was in a trance as he chanted over and over again, 'Dangos y ffordd inni; dangos y ffordd inni; dangos y ffordd inni.'

Jack was frozen to the spot as he watched the boulder sizzle. Soon a crack appeared. It was just big enough for a small boy to squeeze through.

Merlin turned to Jack and said: 'When you pass through the boulder, you will come to a wall of rock. Look carefully and you will see the pattern of a hand carved into the rock. Place your right hand here and the door will open.'

A rush of cold air swirled around Jack. He glanced to his right. Merlin had vanished. Jack's heart thudded in his chest. He was on his own!

Jack felt for the stone around his neck and heard Merlin whispering in his head, 'Remember all that I have told you. Quick, before the opening closes.'

He glanced back one more time and then slid through the gap in the boulder.

Immediately, Jack spotted the hand carved into the rock, so he stepped towards the wall and placed his hand over the rock. A strange prickling sensation shot through his fingers and his palms. Soon, a streak of flashing light shot from each of his fingers and spread out like a shimmering rainbow across the wall. Before long, it began to ripple, and an arched doorway appeared.

Above the doorway was a giant white stone arch. A shiver charged down Jack's back. On top of the archway was painted an enormous dragon, and its massive wings stretched across the whole arch.

'There isn't much time, Jack,' Merlin's voice whispered in his head.

Jack took a deep breath and, without looking back, walked through the door.

THE CAVE

Jack had entered an enormous cave. He stopped at the entrance and took in his surroundings. It was icy cold and turned his breath into misty clouds. Jack's heart pounded in his chest. He saw huge skeletons, skulls and bony limbs scattered across the ground. Above him, stalactites like giant fangs hung from the ceiling. Water trickled down their sides and collected in smooth, shiny pools of ice at the bottom. Across the centre of the cave, huge columns of twisting stone erupted from the floor. Strange writing and symbols covered them from top to bottom.

Jack scanned the walls of the cave looking for the tunnel. Suddenly, he spotted it in the right-hand corner at the back of the cave and started to walk towards it. He had taken no more than a few steps when the light vanished. He spun around and his insides twisted with terror. The door had vanished. He was trapped. Not for the first time, he wondered why he had agreed to this quest.

When he looked across the cave, Jack could only see shimmering shadows and the shapes of the rocky columns rising out of the gloom.

Jack felt for the stone around his neck. He felt a buzzing in his palm and fingers like an electrical current pulsing through his veins. Suddenly, it made him feel brave and strong enough to conquer anything and now he could hear Merlin whispering. 'Use your hands and feet to feel your way.'

It took a moment for Jack's eyes to adjust to the dark. He tried to picture the layout of the cave. To cross the cave to the tunnel, he would have to wind his way between the forest of rocky columns and pray there were no traps he had not spotted. Then, he remembered the pools of ice at the base of the stalactites. Although time was running out, Jack knew he would have to inch his way carefully across the cave.

Slowly, Jack moved across the cave, waving his hands in front of him and sliding his feet cautiously one by one across the floor. With every step, the bones cracked and shattered like dry, dead branches under his feet. Every few steps Jack stopped and listened, but all he could hear was the drip, drip, drip of the water. No sign that the dragon had heard him.

Jack made painfully slow progress. He hadn't gone far but had already scratched his knuckles on the stone columns and bumped his head on the stalactites. Twice, he had stumbled over a bone or rock and crashed to the floor, scraping his hands and knees. 'This is useless. I'll never get to the tunnel,' he said.

A breeze brushed against his face like a cold, thin strip of air and he heard Merlin whispering, 'Let the breeze be your guide, Jack.'

By keeping the breeze in his face, Jack was able to move more quickly across the cave and it was not long before he saw it. A flame flickering in front of him. 'It has to lead to the dragon's den,' Jack thought. 'Now, at least I have some light to guide me.'

The flickering flame grew brighter and brighter, so Jack knew he had to be near the tunnel. And then, the breeze disappeared and was replaced by steaming gusts of hot air. Jack froze and listened for any sound. His eyes darted right and left, trying to pierce the darkness, searching for the slightest movement. Nothing. It was still quiet. He could feel the sweat running down his neck and back. The steaming air was filled with a revolting stench of sulphur and rotten eggs.

Before long, Jack entered a high, circular cavern. In the centre of the cave was an enormous pit. He could hear it bubbling and boiling like tomato soup. He saw it spitting bright red jets of flame and clouds of steam into the air.

The sound of cracking, crushing and crunching echoed around the cave. Jack shrunk back against the wall and held his breath. He watched and waited.

THE DRAGON

All of a sudden, the crunching stopped, and it was silent. The only thing Jack could hear was his heart pounding in his ears. Seconds later, the silence was broken by the swish, swish, swish of a tail across the ground. *'Oh no! It knows I'm here.'* Jack's legs trembled and it took a mighty effort not to run.

A whoosh of stinking air struck Jack in the chest and pinned him against the wall. Sweat dripped down Jack's forehead and into his eyes, but he dared not raise his arm to wipe it away.

The stone throbbed against his chest, and Merlin's warning echoed in his head, 'Stand still. Do not move.'

A deafening boom shook the ground, then another and another. The dragon was coming towards him. Jack could hear its talons clicking on the stone floor. He could smell its stinking breath. His heart hammered in his chest. Still Jack didn't move.

Slowly, Jack raised his right hand towards the stone. When he looked up, the enormous red dragon was towering over him. Its head was bigger than a boulder and it had scales like sharpened steel spikes. Its long tail whipped from side to side.

A sick feeling gurgled in the pit of Jack's stomach. He held his breath as it lowered its head. Its huge emerald green eyes stared at Jack's hand. Jack glanced down. The silver mark was glowing.

The dragon bent closer until its nostrils were nearly touching Jack's face. Still Jack did not move but kept looking into its green eyes. He gripped the stone tighter until he could feel it pressing into his palm and forced himself not to look away.

Jack felt that at any moment his legs would buckle under him and he would be the *dragon desert*. But without warning, the dragon's head suddenly slumped onto its chest and its huge jaw dropped open. Its enormous forked tongue hung out and it dribbled giant strands of slime from the corner of its mouth. Its eyes rolled in its head and then, with an almighty groan, it crashed to the floor. Jack dived to the side just in time.

For what seemed like hours, Jack stood against the wall watching the dragon. 'Now, Jack,' Merlin whispered.

Slowly, Jack moved towards the dragon and knelt at its head. He slid the leather bundle carefully out of his pouch and unfolded it. He was terrified that at any moment it would wake up, so he kept glancing up at the dragon. He could see that it was asleep because its chest gently rose and fell in a steady rhythm.

Jack took a deep breath to block out the stinking stench from the purple paste and stuck his fingers into the putrid slime. He eased the dragon's jaw open wider so he could see the fang. Immediately, he spotted it like a gigantic crystal dewdrop sparkling at him.

Jack had to push through huge strands of dragon drool and his hand soon became slimy and slippery. He had to grit his teeth to stop his stomach heaving. He was glad he hadn't had anything to eat because he was sure he was going to be sick.

Eventually, Jack felt the glassy fang. As quickly as he could, Jack smeared the paste along the gums and sat back.

Within seconds, there was a sizzle and a crack. Quickly, Jack pushed his hand into the dragon's mouth and waited for the fang to drop out. One side of the fang slid out of the gum and dangled down into the dragon's mouth. Jack put his hands under the fang and waited for the other side to drop. Seconds later, it slid into Jack's hands.

It was hard to hold onto the fang because it was covered in slime and slobber and kept slipping out of Jack's hands. With a sigh of relief, Jack wrapped the fang in the strip of leather and carefully placed it in his pouch.

He was just rising to leave when he realised that it had gone quiet. Quickly, he glanced at the dragon. Its chest was still moving up and down. But a prickle spread across Jack's neck. The dragon's eye had flickered briefly. It could be awake any minute. Had he taken too long?

THE ESCAPE

As quick as he could, Jack headed towards the tunnel. He was nearly at the end of the passage when he felt the ground tremble under him. The walls shook and the tunnel echoed with the piercing screech of the dragon. Suddenly, Jack felt a scorching heat on his back. When he spun round, he saw a column of fire tearing down the tunnel towards him. Frantically, he flattened himself against the wall and pressed his palms to his ears to block out the high-pitched shrieks.

The stone throbbed and Jack slid his hand around it. He watched in amazement as the flames burst towards him and then arched away centimetres from covering him in a blanket of fire. Instead, the flames struck the opposite wall and tore down the tunnel.

Jack ran, his arms and legs pumping as he belted down the tunnel. He could see a narrow beam of bright light ahead of him and sprinted towards it. He dodged the rocky columns and ducked under the giant stalactites. All the time, he could hear the dragon's thunderous footsteps and its roar somewhere behind him. Finally, he saw the door in front of him and headed towards it.

He was halfway across the cave when a spear of swirling fire exploded into the cave. It shot towards the ceiling and one after another the stalactites collapsed and crashed to the floor. One shattered at his feet. Jack staggered backwards and tripped over a rock. He fell onto his arm and a terrible pain shot through his body.

For a moment, Jack felt dizzy and sick and he couldn't move. He sat on the ground and hugged his arm to his chest. All around him, rock rained from the ceiling. The thudding was getting nearer and nearer. The ground under him was trembling.

'Get up, Jack. Get up, NOW!' Merlin roared in his head.

Slowly, Jack eased himself up and started to move. A pain shot through his knee, and for a moment Jack's leg buckled under him. Jack gritted his teeth and staggered as fast as he could towards the door. Dazzling sunlight blinded him for a moment. When Jack glanced round, the door had disappeared. All he could hear was the piercing roar of the dragon.

Jack's legs finally gave way and he crashed to the ground. Two ox-hide sandals appeared in front of him and Jack looked up into the beaming face of Merlin. 'Well done, Jack. Only "The Healer" could have got that fang from the dragon. It is your destiny to be the most powerful wizard for good in this land.'

Jack returned to his village a hero. The powder from the dragon's fang saved his parents and his village and rid the country of the killer plague. Over the years, Jack travelled the land healing the sick and destroying the plagues that threatened his country.

34
Modelled sentences

1. THE LEGEND

A. STORY PLOT

Simple statements

- ★ A terrible plague spread throughout the land.
- ★ The only cure was a powder made from a dragon fang.
- ★ Nobody could find the dragon's den.
- ★ Merlin knew Jack could find the cave.
- ★ He told Jack about his quest.
- ★ He instructed him to climb Dragon Ridge Mountain.

Questions

- ★ How were they going to stop the plague**?**
- ★ Who would find the dragon's den**?**

Commands

- ★ **Climb** to the top of Dragon Ridge on the sixth day of the New Moon.

Expanded noun phrases

- ★ **A terrible plague** spread throughout the land.
- ★ They needed a **dragon's crystal fang**.
- ★ Merlin was King Arthur's **famous wizard**.
- ★ Merlin returned from the **mysterious valleys of South Wales**.
- ★ Jack had **a silver birth mark** on his right hand.
- ★ Jack was **a caring, hard-working young boy**.

Similes

★ Jack had a silver **birth mark like a crescent moon**.

Adverbs

★ Merlin had **secretly** taken Jack to live with a family in the north.

Prepositions

★ A terrible plague spread **throughout the land**.
★ People locked themselves **in their homes**.
★ Crops rotted **in the fields**.
★ The dragon's den was **in a cave in the north of the country**.
★ Merlin returned **from the mysterious valleys of South Wales**.
★ Jack had to climb **to the top of Dragon Ridge Mountain**.

Alliteration

★ **d**ragon's **d**en

2. DRAGON RIDGE

A. STORY PLOT

Simple statements

★ It was early morning.
★ It was hard to find the path.
★ Jack remembered the beans in his pocket.
★ The mist parted and he could see the narrow path.
★ Jack started to climb.

Questions

★ How was he going to rescue his village**?**
★ Where was the path**?**
★ When would the mist clear**?**

Exclamations

★ The beans were magic**!**
★ 'Oh no**!**' he gasped.
★ I can't fail now**!**

Commands

★ **Get** moving now.
★ **Use** the beans.

Expanded noun phrases

★ **Brilliant, golden sunshine** lit the top of the mountain.
★ He could see the **icy summit**.
★ A **bubbling stream** tumbled down the mountain.
★ He stared at the **steep, rocky slopes**.
★ An **odd tingling** trickled through his body.
★ It was hidden behind **three big, black boulders**.
★ **Enormous skeletons** covered the floor of the cave.
★ **Huge dark clouds** raced towards the mountain.

Similes

★ He could see the jagged, deadly **peaks like daggers**.
★ The slope was covered in **mist like a white, fleecy blanket**.

Adverbs

★ **Suddenly**, Jack felt an odd tingling trickle through his body.
★ **Immediately**, he could see the inside of the cave.
★ **Quickly**, he felt for the magic beans in his pouch.

Prepositions

★ Jack put his hand **in the pouch**.
★ A disgusting, cheesy smell rose **from the bag**.
★ He threw the magic beans **on the ground**.
★ The entrance to the cave was hidden **behind three huge, black boulders**.
★ **Above him**, Jack heard Merlin's voice.

Dialogue

★ **'Oh no!'** Jack gasped.
★ **'How am I going to rescue the village?'** Jack groaned, slumping against a rock.
★ He could hear Merlin's voice shout, **'Get moving quickly before it is too late.'**

Alliteration

★ **b**ig, **b**lack **b**oulders
★ **t**ingling **t**rickled

3. THE STORM

A. STORY PLOT

Simple statements

★ Jack stepped onto the path.
★ The mist floated above his head.

- ★ Jack trudged on and on.
- ★ He climbed towards the summit.
- ★ He crawled along narrow ledges.
- ★ He scrambled over big black boulders.
- ★ He knew he was getting closer to the top.
- ★ Jack was getting tired.
- ★ The storm had arrived.
- ★ The wind whined and shrieked.
- ★ Thunder crashed and howled.
- ★ The rain hammered on his head.
- ★ He was soaked from head to foot.
- ★ Lightning struck the path.
- ★ A giant crack appeared.
- ★ Jack was trapped.
- ★ There was a loud crack.
- ★ The ledge disappeared.
- ★ Jack tumbled into the dark void below.

Questions

- ★ **Where** are you, Merlin**?**
- ★ **What** do I do now**?**

Exclamations

- ★ Help me**!**

Commands

- ★ **Throw** the beans.
- ★ **Keep** going.

Expanded noun phrases

- ★ He stepped into a **tunnel of swirling, cold mist**.
- ★ He was trapped in a **white woolly blanket of mist**.
- ★ He scrambled towards the **icy summit**.
- ★ He crawled along **narrow ledges**.
- ★ The wind tore the mist into **ragged sheets**.
- ★ **Huge boiling black clouds** raced towards the mountain.
- ★ **An enormous dazzling arrow of lightning** lit up the sky.
- ★ A **loud crack** made him jump out of his skin.
- ★ A **spear of flashing white light spread across the path**.
- ★ A **giant, jagged crack** appeared at his feet.
- ★ Jack tumbled into the **dark void** below.

Similes

- ★ It was **like a giant creature sending its huge icy breaths** down the mountain.
- ★ He clambered over **big black boulders like giant marbles**.
- ★ Lightning **like a flashing spear** lit up the path.
- ★ It was **like being blasted by a fire hose**.

Adverbs

- ★ **Slowly**, he climbed and scrambled towards the icy summit.
- ★ The wind shoved and tugged **fiercely** at him.
- ★ **Suddenly**, Jack stopped.
- ★ **Then**, the lightning struck the path in front of him.
- ★ **Suddenly**, the rock began to crack.

Time conjunctions

- ★ **Hour after hour**, Jack trudged on.
- ★ **First**, a rumble of thunder.
- ★ **Then**, the whistle of the wind.
- ★ **Before long**, the thunder crashed and howled over his head.
- ★ **Then**, lightning like a flashing spear lit up the path.
- ★ **Next** came the rain.

Prepositions

- ★ Jack stepped **into a tunnel** of swirling, cold mist.
- ★ The mist floated **above his head**, curled **around his body** and slithered **over his feet**.
- ★ Big black boulders were scattered **across the path**.
- ★ The wind whistled **around the mountain**.
- ★ The thunder crashed and howled **over his head**.
- ★ Huge boiling black clouds raced **towards the mountain**.
- ★ Rain hammered **on his back**.
- ★ Lightning ripped **through the clouds**.
- ★ Jack tumbled **into the dark void**.

Dialogue

- ★ **'Not far now. Keep going, Jack,'** he kept muttering to himself.
- ★ **'Where are you, Merlin? Help me!'** Jack yelled.
- ★ **'I just want this to be all over. Please, let this nightmare end,'** he sobbed, fighting back the tears.
- ★ Suddenly, the voice inside his head roared, **'Don't move!'**

Alliteration

- ★ **w**hite **w**oolly blanket
- ★ **b**ig **b**lack **b**oulders
- ★ **wh**istle of the **w**ind
- ★ **w**ind **wh**ined
- ★ **b**oiling **b**lack clouds

4. MERLIN

A. STORY PLOT

Simple statements

- ★ Jack tumbled through the air.
- ★ A cloud slid underneath him.
- ★ The cloud drifted towards the mountain.
- ★ The bottom of the cloud slid open.
- ★ Jack slid out of the cloud.
- ★ He was at the entrance to the cave.
- ★ Merlin was waiting for him.
- ★ Merlin waved his bronze staff around Jack to dry his clothes.
- ★ Merlin gave Jack a sweet drink to give him strength.
- ★ Merlin told Jack he had left a roast duck for the dragon.
- ★ He had sprinkled a sleeping potion on the roast duck.
- ★ Merlin gave Jack a pink stone on a leather thread.
- ★ Merlin could use the stone to help Jack.
- ★ Jack had to find the cave with the enormous pit in the centre.
- ★ The dragon was in this cave.
- ★ Merlin told Jack to show the dragon his hand and look him in the eye.
- ★ He gave Jack a paste to rub on the dragon's gums.
- ★ The paste would make the crystal fang drop out.

Questions

- ★ Do you feel better now?
- ★ Will the dragon be awake?
- ★ What do I do if the dragon sees me?
- ★ How do I extract the crystal fang?
- ★ What do I do if it wakes up?
- ★ Aren't you coming with me?

Exclamations

- ★ Crows Claws!
- ★ I can't do this!

Commands

- ★ **Down** in one.
- ★ **Listen** carefully.
- ★ **Wear** this.
- ★ **Hold** the crystal in your right hand.
- ★ **Wait** until the dragon is asleep.

Expanded noun phrases

- ★ Jack felt **a fleecy pillow** slide underneath him.
- ★ The **cold and damp** from his **sodden clothes** had seeped into his bones.
- ★ He squeezed out his **wet tunic**.
- ★ Merlin's **long white hair and beard** blew in the wind.
- ★ Jack lifted the **wooden tankard** to his **dry lips**.
- ★ He took a **tiny sip**.
- ★ He pointed at **the silver mark** on Jack's right hand.
- ★ Merlin raised his **huge bronze staff**.
- ★ **A hot wind** gusted around Jack.
- ★ Merlin put his hand inside his **long, woollen cloak**.
- ★ He pulled out **a wooden tankard**.
- ★ **A delicious sweet taste** flooded his mouth.
- ★ There is **an enormous pit** in the centre of the cave.
- ★ Merlin dug inside his **blue cloak** and pulled out **a small leather bundle**.

Similes

- ★ It looked **like a giant ball of cotton wool**.
- ★ The cloud vanished **like a puff of smoke**.
- ★ Energy raced through Jack's body **like an electric current**.

Adverbs

- ★ Jack spun **wildly** head over heels.
- ★ The cloud was drifting **slowly** beneath him.
- ★ **Suddenly**, the movement stopped.
- ★ Jack shivered **uncontrollably**.
- ★ Merlin moved his bronze staff **slowly** around Jack.
- ★ A hot wind gusted around Jack's legs, **then** his body and **finally**, his arms and head.
- ★ … Merlin said **kindly**.
- ★ **Slowly**, Jack lifted the tankard to his dry lips.
- ★ The dragon should be asleep **soon**.
- ★ Merlin unwrapped the leather bundle **carefully**.
- ★ Jack **quickly** raised his head.

★ The fang will drop out **rapidly**.
★ **Suddenly**, Merlin stood up.

Prepositions

★ Jack spun head over heels **through the air**.
★ His eyes were bulging **out of their sockets**.
★ He tumbled **towards the ground**.
★ He felt a fleecy pillow slide **underneath him**.
★ All **around him** was brilliant white.
★ He was **at the entrance to the dragon's cave**.
★ Merlin's voice boomed out **across the mountain**.
★ The cold and damp had seeped **into his bones**.
★ Merlin towered **over him**.
★ Merlin put an arm **around Jack's shoulder**.
★ Merlin guided Jack **towards a boulder**.
★ He sat down **beside Jack**.
★ The smell of cinnamon and honey wafted **up Jack's nose**.
★ Merlin pulled a pink stone **out of his cloak**.
★ 'You will see a tunnel **ahead of you**.'
★ Rub the paste **onto the dragon's gums**.
★ Jack slid the bundle **into the pouch around his waist**.

Dialogue

★ **'I thought I was too late**,' Merlin's voice boomed out across the mountain.
★ **'You need to get your strength back**,' Merlin said, guiding Jack towards a boulder.
★ **'You'll feel better once you have something warm inside you**,' Merlin said kindly.
★ **'Thank you, Merlin**,' Jack said, handing the tankard back to the wizard.
★ **'Crows' Claws! Do you mean the dragon might wake up?'** Jack said, his eyes wide with fear.
★ **'I can't do this**,' he said, shaking his head.
★ Jack took a deep breath. **'But what do I do if it wakes up?'**
★ **'So many questions**,' Merlin chuckled.
★ **'If you are with me, I will try**,' Jack said quietly.
★ **'This is where you will find the dragon.'** Merlin paused to make sure Jack had understood his instructions.
★ **'What will happen if I look away?'** Jack whispered.
★ **'You will no longer be protected**,' Merlin replied.

Alliteration

★ **C**rows' **c**laws
★ **b**eetles, **b**ats and **b**itter **b**erries

5. THE PORTAL

A. STORY PLOT

Simple statements

- ★ Merlin opened a narrow crack in the boulder.
- ★ Jack had to look for a hand carved into the rock.
- ★ Merlin vanished.
- ★ Jack put his hand onto the rock.
- ★ A doorway appeared.
- ★ Jack walked through the door.

Questions

- ★ How do I get into the cave**?**
- ★ Where's the hand**?**

Exclamations

- ★ Sizzling snakes**!**
- ★ What have I agreed to**!**
- ★ He was on his own**!**

Commands

- ★ **Stand** in front of the centre boulder.
- ★ **Show** this boy the way.
- ★ **Look** carefully for the pattern of a hand.
- ★ **Place** your right hand on this rock.
- ★ **Remember** all that I have told you.

Expanded noun phrases

- ★ Merlin grasped his **bronze staff** in both hands.
- ★ **A bright light** glowed from the end of **the bronze staff**.
- ★ **A rush of cold air** swirled around Jack.
- ★ **A strange prickling sensation** shot through his fingers and palm.
- ★ **A streak of flashing light** exploded from his fingers.
- ★ Above the doorway was **a giant white stone arch.**
- ★ **An enormous red dragon** was painted on top of the arch.
- ★ **Its massive wings** stretched across the arch.
- ★ Jack took **a deep breath**.

Similes

- ★ Merlin's cloak flapped **like giant wings** around him.
- ★ A flashing light spread out **like a shimmering rainbow** across the wall.

Adverbs

- ★ Merlin **slowly** rocked backwards and forwards.
- ★ **Soon**, a crack appeared.
- ★ Look **carefully.**
- ★ **Immediately**, Jack spotted the hand carved into the rock.

Prepositions

- ★ 'Stand **in front of the centre boulder.'**
- ★ Jack glanced **to his right.**
- ★ Merlin raised his bronze staff **above his head.**
- ★ His voice echoed **around the mountain.**
- ★ A bright light glowed **from the end of the staff.**
- ★ Merlin's cloak flapped **around him.**
- ★ Pass **through the boulder.**
- ★ He glanced **to his right.**
- ★ His heart thudded **in his chest.**
- ★ He stepped **towards the wall.**
- ★ He placed his hand **over the rock.**
- ★ A strange prickling sensation shot **through his fingers.**
- ★ **Above the doorway** was a giant white stone arch.
- ★ A shiver charged **down Jack's back.**
- ★ **On top of the archway** was painted an enormous dragon.

Dialogue

- ★ **'Stand in front of the centre boulder,'** Merlin told Jack.
- ★ He chanted over and over again, **'Dangos y ffordd inni.'**
- ★ He heard Merlin whispering in his head, **'Remember all that I have told you.'**

Alliteration

- ★ **s**trange **s**ensation

6. THE CAVE

A. STORY PLOT

Simple statements

- ★ Jack entered an enormous cave.
- ★ There were huge skeletons all over the floor.
- ★ He saw the tunnel in the corner of the cave.
- ★ The door closed behind him.
- ★ It was very dark.
- ★ Jack had to go around enormous rocky columns.

★ He moved across the dark cave slowly.
★ Merlin sent a breeze to guide him.

Questions

★ Where is the tunnel**?**

Exclamations

★ I'll never get out of here**!**
★ Boars' Bottom**!**

Commands

★ **Use** your hands and feet.
★ **Let** the breeze be your guide.

Expanded noun phrases

★ It was **icy cold**.
★ He saw **huge skeletons, skulls and bony limbs** on the ground.
★ There were **smooth, shiny pools of ice** at the bottom of the stalactites.
★ **Huge columns of twisting stone** erupted from the floor.
★ **Strange writing and ancient symbols** covered the columns.
★ Jack could only see **shimmering shadows** and the shapes of the **rocky columns**.
★ He had to wind his way between the **forest of rocky columns**.
★ Jack made **slow progress**.
★ **A cold breeze** brushed against his face.
★ The breeze was replaced by **steaming gusts of hot air**.
★ The air was filled with **a revolting stench of sulphur and rotten eggs**.
★ Jack entered **a high circular cavern**.
★ **Spitting red jets of flame** shot into the air.

Similes

★ His breath was **like misty clouds**.
★ Stalactites **like giant fangs** hung from the ceiling.
★ He felt a buzzing in his fingers **like an electrical current pulsing through his veins**.
★ The bones shattered and cracked **like dry, dead bones** under his feet.
★ A breeze brushed against his face **like a draught from an open door**.
★ The pit boiled and bubbled **like tomato soup**.

Adverbs

- ★ **Suddenly**, he spotted the tunnel in the corner of the cave.
- ★ **Slowly**, Jack moved across the wave.
- ★ He slid his feet **cautiously** one by one across the floor.
- ★ Jack made **painfully** slow progress.

Prepositions

- ★ Jack stopped **at the entrance**.
- ★ His heart pounded **in his chest**.
- ★ Skeletons, skulls and limbs were scattered **across the ground**.
- ★ Huge stalactites hung **from the ceiling**.
- ★ Water trickled **down the sides of the stalactites**.
- ★ Columns of twisting stone erupted **from the floor**.
- ★ He spotted it **at the back of the cave**.
- ★ He looked **across the cave**.
- ★ Rocky columns rose **out of the gloom**.
- ★ He felt for the stone **around his neck**.
- ★ He had to wind his way **between the rocky columns**.
- ★ Jack waved his hands **in front of him**.
- ★ The bones cracked and shattered **under his feet**.
- ★ He scratched his knuckles **on the stone columns**.
- ★ He bumped his head **on the stalactites**.
- ★ He stumbled **over a bone**.
- ★ He crashed **to the floor**.
- ★ A breeze brushed **against his face**.

Dialogue

- ★ **'Use your hands and feet to feel the way**,' the voice whispered.
- ★ **'This is useless**,' Jack groaned.
- ★ He heard Merlin whispering, **'Let the breeze be your guide, Jack.'**
- ★ **'It has to lead to the dragon's den**,' Jack thought. **'Now, at least I have some light to guide me.'**

Alliteration

- ★ **s**keletons and **s**kulls
- ★ **t**wisted with **t**error
- ★ **sh**immering **sh**adows
- ★ **b**reeze **b**rushed
- ★ **B**oars' **B**ottom!
- ★ **f**lickering **f**lame
- ★ **c**racking, **c**rushing, **c**runching

7. THE DRAGON

A. STORY PLOT

Simple statements

- ★ The dragon knew Jack was there.
- ★ The dragon came closer.
- ★ Jack stood very still.
- ★ He looked into the dragon's eyes.
- ★ The dragon collapsed onto the floor.
- ★ The dragon was asleep.
- ★ Jack rubbed the paste onto the dragon's gums.
- ★ The fang dropped out.
- ★ Jack put the fang into his pouch.
- ★ The dragon's eye flickered.
- ★ It would be awake any moment.

Questions

Is it asleep**?**

Had he taken too long**?**

Exclamations

- ★ Oh no**!** It knows I'm here!

Commands

- ★ **Stand** absolutely still.
- ★ **Do not** move a muscle.

Expanded noun phrases

- ★ **A whoosh of stinking air** struck Jack in the chest.
- ★ **A deafening boom** shook the ground.
- ★ He could smell its **stinking breath**.
- ★ The **enormous red dragon** towered over him.
- ★ Its **long, barbed tail** whipped from side to side.
- ★ A **horrible sick feeling** gurgled in the pit of Jack's stomach.
- ★ Its **huge emerald green eyes** stared at Jack's hand.
- ★ The **silver mark** glowed.
- ★ Its **massive jaw** dropped open.
- ★ Its **enormous forked tongue** hung out.
- ★ It dribbled **giant slimy strands of slobber**.
- ★ **A stinking stench** rose from the **purple paste**.

★ There were **huge strands of dragon drool**.
★ He couldn't hold on to the **slimy, slippery fang**.

Similes

★ It had **scales like sharpened spikes**.
★ The fang was **like a gigantic crystal dewdrop**.

Adverbs

★ **All of a sudden**, the crunching stopped.
★ **Seconds later**, the silence was broken by the swish, swish, swish of a tail.
★ He blinked **rapidly**.
★ Its nostrils were **nearly** touching Jack's face.
★ The dragon's head **suddenly** slumped onto its chest.
★ Jack moved **slowly** towards the dragon.
★ He slid the leather bundle **carefully** out of his pouch.
★ Its chest was **gently** rising and falling.
★ **Eventually**, he felt the glassy fang.
★ **As quickly as he could**, Jack smeared the paste along the gums.
★ **Within seconds**, there was a sizzle and a crack.
★ **Quickly**, Jack pushed his hand into the dragon's mouth.
★ The dragon's eye flickered **briefly**.

Prepositions

★ His heart pounded **in his ears**.
★ There was a swish, swish of a tail **across the ground**.
★ A whoosh of air pinned Jack **against the wall**.
★ Merlin's warning echoed **in his head**.
★ The dragon was coming **towards him**.
★ The enormous dragon was towering **over him**.
★ Its tail whipped **from side to side**.
★ Jack looked **into its green eyes**.
★ He thought his legs would buckle **under him**.
★ It dribbled giant strands of slime **from the corner of its mouth**.
★ He dived **to the side**.
★ He stood **against the wall**.
★ He pushed his hand **through huge strands of dragon drool**.
★ He smeared the paste **along the gums**.
★ The slimy fang slipped **out of his hands**.

Dialogue

★ '**Now, Jack**,' Merlin whispered.

Alliteration

- ★ **s**cales like **s**harpened **s**pikes
- ★ **d**ragon's **d**esert
- ★ **st**rands of **sl**ime
- ★ **st**inking **st**ench
- ★ **d**ragon **d**rool
- ★ **sl**ime and **sl**obber

8. ESCAPE

A. STORY PLOT

Simple statements

- ★ Jack headed towards the tunnel.
- ★ The dragon heard him.
- ★ The dragon sent a column of fire down the tunnel.
- ★ The stone made it bounce off the wall away from Jack.
- ★ Jack sprinted down the tunnel.
- ★ The dragon chased after Jack.
- ★ The dragon set fire to the ceiling.
- ★ Rocks rained down on top of Jack.
- ★ Jack fell to the floor.
- ★ He hurt his arm and leg.
- ★ The doorway opened.
- ★ Jack staggered out of the door.
- ★ Merlin was waiting for him.

Questions

- ★ Where is it**?**
- ★ What's that smell**?**

Exclamations

- ★ It's awake**!**

Commands

- ★ **Get up**, NOW.

Expanded noun phrases

- ★ The **dragon's piercing screech** echoed around the tunnel.
- ★ He felt a **scorching heat** on his back.
- ★ **A column of bright red fire** tore down the tunnel.
- ★ They were going to cover him in a **blanket of fire**.

* He saw **a narrow beam of light**.
* He ducked under the **giant jagged stalactites**.
* He could hear the **dragon's thunderous footsteps**.
* A **spear of swirling fire** exploded into the cave.
* A **terrible pain** shot through his body.
* **Dazzling sunlight** blinded him.
* He could hear the **piercing roar of the dragon**.

Similes

* He felt the ground shake **like an earthquake** beneath him.

Adverbs

* **As quickly as he could**, Jack headed for the tunnel.
* **Suddenly**, Jack felt a scorching heat on his back.
* **Frantically**, he flattened himself against the wall.
* **Finally**, he saw the doorway.
* **For a moment**, he felt dizzy and sick.
* Jack eased himself **slowly** up onto his feet.
* Jack's legs **finally** gave way.

Prepositions

* Jack headed **towards the tunnel**.
* The ground **shook under his feet**.
* He felt a scorching heat **on his back**.
* A column of fire tore **down the tunnel towards him**.
* He flattened himself **against the wall**.
* He pressed his hands **to his ears**.
* He saw a narrow beam of light **ahead of him**.
* The dragon was somewhere **behind him**.
* A spear of swirling fire shot **towards the ceiling**.
* The stalactites crashed **to the floor**.
* Jack tripped **over a rock**.
* He fell **onto his arm**.
* A terrible pain shot **through his body**.
* He hugged his arm **to his chest**.
* A pain shot **through his knee**.
* Jack looked **up into Merlin's beaming face**.

DIALOGUE

* '**Well done, Jack!**' Merlin said, beaming.

Alliteration

* **s**pear of **s**wirling fire

35
Innovating sentences model

STATEMENTS			
It	**was**	**early**	**morning**.
It	was		.
It was	**hard to find**	**the path**	**to the dragon's cave.**
It was	hard to find	the path	.
It was	hard to find		to the dragon's cave.
Jack	**remembered**	**the beans**	**in his pouch.**
Jack	remembered		in his pouch.
Jack	remembered	the beans	.
He	**could see**	**the narrow path**	**up the mountain.**
He	could see	the narrow path	.
He	could see		up the mountain.
Jack	**started**	**to climb**	**up the mountain.**
Jack	started		up the mountain.
Jack	started	to climb	.

QUESTIONS	
How was he going to	**rescue his village?**
How was he going to	?
Where was	**the path?**
Where was	?

Where was		?
When would	**the mist clear?**	
When would		?
Why did they	**choose him?**	
Why did they		?

EXCLAMATIONS

The	beans	were	magic!
The		were	magic!
'Oh	no!'	he	gasped.
'	!'	he	gasped.
'Oh	no!'	he	.
I	can't	fail	now!
I	can't		now!

COMMANDS

Get	moving	now.
Get		now.
Get	moving	.
Look	up.	
Look	.	
	up.	
Use	the	beans.
	the	beans.
Use	the	.

EXPANDED NOUN PHRASES AND SIMILES

Brilliant	golden	sunshine	lit	the top of the mountain.
		sunshine	lit	the top of the mountain.
Brilliant			lit	the top of the mountain.
			covered	the top of the mountain.
Brilliant	golden	sunshine		.

He	could see	the	icy	summit.	
He	could see	the		summit.	
He	could see	the			.
He	**stared at**	**the**	**steep**	**rocky**	**slopes.**
He	stared at	the			slopes.
He	stared at	the			.
He		the	steep	rocky	slopes.
A	**bubbling**	**stream**	**tumbled**	**down the mountain.**	
A		stream	tumbled	down the mountain.	
A	bubbling	stream	tumbled		.
A	bubbling	stream		down the mountain.	
An	**odd**	**tingling**	**trickled**	**through his body.**	
A		tingling	trickled	through his body.	
A			trickled	through his body.	
An	odd	tingling	trickled		.
An	odd	tingling		through his body.	
The	**beans**	**felt**	**warm**	**and**	**hairy.**
The	beans	felt		and	.
The		felt	warm	and	hairy.
Enormous	skeletons	covered	the	floor	of the cave.
Enormous	skeletons	covered	the		
	skeletons	covered	the	floor	of the cave.
Enormous		covered	the	floor	of the cave.
Huge	**dark**	**clouds**	**raced**	**towards the mountain.**	
Huge	dark	clouds		towards the mountain.	
		clouds	raced	towards the mountain.	
Huge	dark		raced	towards the mountain.	
Huge	dark	clouds	raced		.

SIMILES

He	could see	jagged	deadly	peaks	like daggers.
He	could see			peaks	like daggers.
He	could see	jagged	deadly	peaks	like .
Mist	**like a fleecy white blanket**	**covered**	**the**	**slope.**	
Mist	like a fleecy white blanket	covered	the		.
Mist	like	covered	the	slope.	

ADVERBS

Suddenly	**Jack**	**felt**	**an**	**odd**	**tingling.**
	Jack	felt	an	odd	tingling.
Suddenly	Jack	felt	a		.
Immediately	**he**	**could see**	**the**	**inside of the cave.**	
	he	could see	the	inside of the cave.	
Immediately	he	could see			.
Immediately	he	could **hear**			.
Quickly	**he**	**felt for**	**the magic beans**	**in his pouch.**	
	he	felt for the	the magic beans	in his pouch.	
Quickly	he	felt for the		in his pouch.	

PREPOSITIONS

Jack	put	his	hand	in his pouch.
Jack	put	his	hand	.
Jack	put			.
A	disgusting	cheesy	smell	rose from the bag.
A	disgusting	cheesy	smell	.
A			smell	rose from the bag.
He	**threw**	**the**	**magic beans**	**on the ground.**
He	threw	the	magic beans	.

He	threw	the		on the ground.
The	**entrance to the**	**cave**	**was hidden**	**behind big black boulders.**
The	entrance to the	cave	was hidden	.
The	entrance to the		was hidden	behind .
Above him	Jack	heard	Merlin's	voice.
	Jack	heard	Merlin's	voice.
Above him	Jack	heard		.

36

Coordination and subordination

Clause (1)	Conjunction	Clause (2)	√
There was a terrible plague	**and**	a. only a crystal dragon fang could cure it.	
		b. towns and villages had a wonderful harvest.	
The dragon lived in a cave	**and**	a. no-one ever found it.	
		b. was known as The Great Dragon of the North.	
King Arthur's knight searched and searched	**but**	a. no-one ever found it.	
		b. found it on a special map.	
Merlin knew the location of the dragon's den	**but**	a. he also knew only Jack would be able to enter the cave.	
		b. he told King Arthur.	
Jack had to climb the mountain	**and**	a. find the cave.	
		b. meet Merlin at the top.	
Every village had the fever and sickness	**so**	a. people locked themselves in their homes.	
		b. all work had stopped.	
People locked themselves in their homes	**because**	a. the crops rotted in the fields.	
		a. there was a terrible plague.	

36 *'Language in action': coordination/subordination*

EXERCISE 1: COMBINING THE PHRASES INTO SENTENCES AND INTO A PARAGRAPH

Using *and*, *but*, *because* and *so* to develop sentence structure.
Complete the following sentence stems:

There was a terrible plague **and**_____

The dragon lived in a cave **and**_____

King Arthur's knights searched and searched, **but**_____

Merlin knew the location of the dragon's den, **but**_____

Jack had to climb the mountain **and**_____

Every village had the fever and sickness, **so**_____

People locked themselves in their homes **because**_____

Examples

There was a terrible plague **and** only a crystal dragon fang could cure it.

The dragon lived in a cave **and** was known as the Great Dragon of the North.

King Arthur's knights searched and searched, **but** no-one ever found it.

Merlin knew the location of the dragon's den, **but** he also knew only Jack would be able to enter the cave.

Jack had to climb the mountain **and** meet Merlin at the top.

Every village had the fever and sickness, **so** people locked themselves in their homes.

People locked themselves in their homes **because** there was a terrible plague.

DRAGON RIDGE MOUNTAIN

Clause (1)	Conjunction	Clause (2)	√
It was early morning	**and**	a. the top of the mountain was lit by brilliant golden sunshine.	
		b. the top of the mountain was lit by brilliant silver starlight.	
Jack squinted into the sun	**and**	a. opened his eyes.	
		b. looked for the path to the dragon's cave.	
He could see the icy summit	**and**	a. his mother and father.	
		b. the jagged, deadly peaks like daggers.	
He stared at the steep, rocky slopes	**but**	a. he could not see the entrance to the cave.	
		b. he could see the entrance to the cave.	

It was hard to find the path	**because**	a. he kept on looking.	
		b. the slope was covered in mist.	
Jack groaned	**and**	a. slumped against a rock.	
		b. started to dance.	
Jack didn't know how the beans could help	**but**	a. he had no other plan.	
		b. he didn't like beans.	
The beans felt warm and hairy	**and**	a. a wonderful sweet smell rose from the pouch.	
		b. a disgusting cheesy smell rose from the pouch.	
He could not see or hear the dragon	**but**	a. he could see its huge claws.	
		b. he could smell smoke and burning flesh.	
Jack knew there was no time to lose	**so**	a. he started to climb.	
		b. he sat down on a rock.	

EXERCISE 2: COMBINING THE PHRASES INTO SENTENCES AND INTO A PARAGRAPH

Using *and, but, because* and *so* to develop sentence structure.
Complete the following sentence stems:

It was early morning **and**_____

Jack squinted into the sun **and**_____

He could see the icy summit, **but**_____

He stared at the steep, rocky slopes, **but**_____

It was hard to find the path **because**_____

Jack groaned **and** _____

Jack didn't know how the beans would help, **but**_____

The beans felt warm and hairy **and**_____

He could not see or hear the dragon, **but**_____

Jack knew that there was no time to lose, **so**_____

Examples

It was early morning **and** the top of the mountain was lit by brilliant golden sunshine.

Jack squinted into the sun **and** looked for the path to the dragon's cave.

He could see the icy summit above him **and** the jagged, deadly peaks like daggers.

He stared at the steep, rocky slopes, **but** he could not see the entrance to the cave.

It was hard to find the path **because** the slope was covered in mist.

Jack groaned **and** slumped against a rock.

Jack didn't know how the beans could help, **but** he had no other plan.

The beans felt warm and hairy **and** a disgusting cheesy smell rose from the pouch.

He could not see or hear the dragon, **but** he could smell smoke and burning flesh.

Jack knew there was no time to lose, **so** he started to climb.

THE STORM

Clause (1)	Conjunction	Clause (2)	√
Jack stepped onto the path	**and**	a. into a tunnel of swirling cold mist.	
		b. went through the door.	
The mist floated above his head	**and**	a. hit him in the face.	
		b. slithered over his feet.	
He didn't know if he could climb much further	**but**	a. the thought of his parents urged him on.	
		b. blisters exploded on his feet.	
The rain hammered on his back	**and**	a. he did not get wet.	
		b. stung his face.	
Jack wasn't sure he would make it	**but**	a. he gritted his teeth.	
		b. he was exhausted.	
The wind tugged at Jack	**and**	a. he struggled to stay on his feet.	
		b. he kept climbing.	
The rain hammered on his back	**and**	a. stung his face.	
		b. soaked him head to foot.	
It was hard to walk	**and**	a. he was nearly there.	
		b. he wasn't sure he would make it.	
It was hard to breathe	**so**	a. Jack was exhausted.	
		b. he ran the rest of the way.	
Jack looked up	**and**	a. closed his eyes.	
		b. froze.	

Lightning ripped through the clouds	**and**	a. lit up the dragon's den.	
		b. struck the path in front of him.	
Jack took a deep breath	**and**	a. fell to his knees.	
		b. pressed his back against the mountain.	
He was trapped	**because**	a. the ledge started to crack.	
		b. he had nowhere to run to.	
The ledge disappeared	**as**	a. he fell into the dark void.	
		b. he tumbled through the air.	

EXERCISE 3: COMBINING THE PHRASES INTO SENTENCES AND INTO A PARAGRAPH

Using *and, but, because* and *so* to develop sentence structure.
Complete the following sentence stems:

Jack stepped onto the path **and**_____

The mist floated above his head **and**_____

He didn't know if he could climb much further, **but**_____

The rain hammered on his back **and**_____

Jack wasn't sure he would make it, **but**_____

Jack put his hands to his face **and**_____

The wind tugged at Jack **and** _____

The rain hammered on his back **and** _____

It was hard to walk **and** _____

Jack looked up **and**_____

The rock began to ripple **and**_____

Lightning ripped through the clouds **and** _____

He was trapped **because** _____

The ledge disappeared **and** _____

Examples

Jack stepped onto the path **and** into a tunnel of swirling cold mist.

The mist floated above his head **and** slithered over his feet.

He didn't know if he could climb much further, **but** the thought of his parents urged him on.

The rain hammered on his back **and** stung his face.

Jack wasn't sure he would make it, **but** he gritted his teeth and kept on climbing.

The wind tugged at Jack **and** he struggled to stay on his feet.

The rain hammered on his back **and** stung his face.

177

It was hard to walk **and** he wasn't sure he would make it.

It was hard to breathe **so** Jack was exhausted.

Jack looked up **and** froze.

Lightning ripped through the clouds **and** struck the path in front of him.

Jack took a deep breath **and** pressed his back against the mountain.

He was trapped **because** the ledge started to crack all around him.

The ledge disappeared **and** he tumbled through the air.

MERLIN

Clause (1)	Conjunction	Clause (2)	√
Jack braced himself for the impact with the ground	**but**	a. he struck his head.	
		a. it never came.	
He was at the entrance	**and**	a. the dragon was waiting for him.	
		b. Merlin was waiting for him.	
Merlin raised his bronze staff	**and**	a. he could see Jack.	
		b. moved it slowly around Jack.	
Merlin put his hand inside his cloak	**and**	a. pulled out a wooden tankard.	
		b. warmed his hands.	
Jack was very thirsty	**so**	a. he drunk it down in one gulp.	
		b. he didn't want to drink.	
The roast duck had gone	**so**	a. there's nothing for lunch.	
		b. the dragon should be asleep soon.	
The sleeping potion is a new recipe	**so**	a. I'm not sure how long it will last.	
		b. the other one didn't work.	
Jack leant over to look at the paste	**but**	a. smelled the paste.	
		b. quickly raised his head.	
It doesn't smell good	**but**	a. it is made of beetles, bats and bitter berries.	
		b. it will work.	
The fang will drop out rapidly	**so**	a. make sure you are ready.	
		b. there will be no warning.	

Merlin stared at Jack	**and**	a. then pulled out a pink stone.	
		b. gave him a pebble.	
He leant over	**and**	a. whispered into Jack's ear.	
		b. hung the stone around Jack's neck.	
I cannot enter the cave	**but**	a. the stone is my eyes and ears.	
		b. I cannot get through the narrow crack.	
Merlin stood up	**and**	a. vanished.	
		b. beckoned for Jack to follow him.	
Jack realized he was surrounded by a cloud	**when**	a. he opened his eyes.	
		b. it stopped moving.	
The cloud had vanished	**when**	a. it was like a puff of smoke.	
		b. he looked up.	
You need to get your strength back	**before**	a. you face the dragon.	
		b. your climb.	
You will see a tunnel ahead of you	**when**	a. you see the dragon.	
		b. you enter the cave.	
Follow this tunnel	**until**	a. it leads you to the dragon.	
		b. you come to a second cave.	
I am not sure how long the sleeping potion will last	**because**	a. it's a new recipe.	
		b. it's revolting.	

EXERCISE 4: COMBINING THE PHRASES INTO SENTENCES AND INTO A PARAGRAPH

Using *and, but, because, so, when, before, until* to develop sentence structure.
Complete the following sentence stems:

Jack braced himself for the impact, **but**_____

He was at the entrance **and**_____

Merlin raised his bronze staff **and**_____

Merlin put his hand inside his cloak **and**_____

Jack was very thirsty, **so**_____

The roast duck had gone, **so**_____

The sleeping potion is a new recipe, **so**_____

Jack leant over to look at the paste, **but**_____

It doesn't smell good, **but**_____

The fang will drop out rapidly, **so**_____

Merlin stared at Jack **and**_____

He leant over **and**_____

I cannot enter the cave, **but**_____

Merlin stood up **and**_____

Jack realised he was surrounded by a cloud **when**_____

The cloud had vanished **when**_____

You need to get your strength back **before**_____

You will see a tunnel ahead of you **when**_____

Follow this tunnel **until**_____

I am not sure how long the sleeping potion will last **because**_____

Examples

Jack braced himself for the impact, **but** it never came.

He was at the entrance **and** Merlin was waiting for him.

Merlin raised his bronze staff **and** moved it slowly around Jack.

Merlin put his hand inside his cloak **and** pulled out a wooden tankard.

Jack was very thirsty, **so** he drank it down in one gulp.

The roast duck had gone, **so** the dragon should be asleep soon.

The sleeping potion is a new recipe, **so** I'm not sure how long it will last.

Jack leant over to look at the paste, **but** quickly raised his head.

It doesn't smell good, **but** it will work.

The fang will drop out rapidly, **so** make sure you are ready.

Merlin stared at Jack **and** then pulled out a pink stone.

He leant over **and** hung the stone around Jack's neck.

I cannot enter the cave, **but** the stone is my eyes and ears.

Merlin stood up **and** beckoned for Jack to follow him.

Jack realized he was surrounded by a cloud **when** he opened his eyes.

The cloud had vanished **when** he looked up.

You need to get your strength back **before** you face the dragon.

You will see a tunnel ahead of you **when** you enter the cave.

Follow this tunnel **until** you come to a second cave.

I am not sure how long the sleeping potion will last **because** it's a new recipe.

THE PORTAL

Clause (1)	Conjunction	Clause (2)	√
Merlin closed his eyes	**and**	a. nodded off.	
		b. rocked backwards and forwards.	
Jack turned to talk to Merlin	**but**	a. he had vanished.	
		b. asked him what he should do next.	
Jack felt for the stone around his neck	**and**	a. heard Merlin whispering in his head.	
		b. he knew it would help him.	
Jack glanced back one more time	**and**	a. slid through the gap.	
		b. he wanted to look at the mountain.	
The crack was narrow	**so**	a. Merlin could not go with Jack.	
		b. he could pass through the boulder.	
Jack spotted the hand carved into the rock	**so**	a. he didn't know what to do next.	
		b. he placed his hand on this spot.	
A streak of flashing light shot from his fingers	**and**	a. spread out like a shimmering rainbow across the wall.	
		b. the mark on his hand was magic.	
The wall began to ripple	**and**	a. he walked through the doorway.	
		b. an arched doorway appeared.	
Merlin lowered his staff onto the boulder	**when**	a. it stopped glowing.	
		b. the wind had died down.	
Merlin could not go with Jack	**because**	a. the crack was too narrow.	
		b. he had vanished.	
The rock began to ripple	**and**	a. a door appeared.	
		b. raced towards the mountain.	

EXERCISE 5: COMBINING THE PHRASES INTO SENTENCES AND INTO A PARAGRAPH

Using *and, but, because, so* and *when* to develop sentence structure.
Complete the following sentence stems:

Merlin closed his eyes **and**_____

Jack turned to talk to Merlin, **but**_____

Jack felt for the stone around his neck **and**_____

Jack glanced back one more time **and**_____

The crack was narrow, **so**_____

Jack spotted the hand carved into the rock, **so**_____

A streak of flashing light shot from his fingers **and**_____

The wall began to ripple **and**_____

Merlin lowered his staff onto the boulder **when**_____

Merlin could not go with Jack **because**_____

The rock began to ripple **and**_____

Examples

Merlin closed his eyes **and** rocked backwards and forwards.

Jack turned to talk to Merlin, **but** he had vanished.

Jack felt for the stone around his neck **and** heard Merlin whispering in his head.

Jack glanced back one more time **and** slid through the gap.

The crack was narrow, **so** Merlin could not go with Jack.

Jack spotted the hand carved into the rock, **so** he placed his hand on this spot.

A streak of flashing light shot from his fingers **and** spread out like a shimmering rainbow across the wall.

The wall began to ripple, **and** an arched doorway appeared.

Merlin lowered his staff onto the boulder **when** the wind had died down.

Merlin could not go with Jack **because** the crack was too narrow.

The rock began to ripple, **and** a door appeared.

THE CAVE

Clause (1)	Conjunction	Clause (2)	√
Jack stopped at the entrance	**and**	a. took in his surroundings.	
		b. looked around.	
It was icy cold	**and**	a. Jack was still hot.	
		b. turned his breath into misty clouds.	
Water trickled down the stalactites	**and**	a. collected in smooth, shiny pools of ice.	
		b. there were cracks in the ceiling.	
Jack spotted the tunnel in the corner	**and**	a. didn't know how he would cross the cave in the dark.	
		b. walked towards it.	

He spun around	**and**	a. his insides twisted with terror.	
		b. he heard a noise.	
Jack waved his hands in front of him	**and**	a. slid his feet across the floor.	
		b. he could feel his way.	
Jack stopped and listened	**but**	a. heard the water dripping down the walls.	
		b. all he could hear was the drip, drip, drip of the water.	
He hadn't gone far	**but**	a. he was going so slowly.	
		b. had already scratched his knuckles and bumped his head.	
He stumbled over a rock	**and**	a. crashed to the floor.	
		b. he couldn't see it in the dark.	
There were pools of ice at the base of the stalactites	**so**	a. the water had dripped down them.	
		b. he knew he would have to move carefully.	
He had only taken a few steps	**when**	a. the light vanished.	
		b. he wanted to turn back.	
Jack could only see shimmering shadows	**when**	a. he looked across the cave.	
		b. there was very little light.	
It was a treacherous, winding path between the rocky columns	**so**	a. he went as fast as he could.	
		b. he prayed there were no traps he had not spotted.	
It was pitch black in the cave	**because**	a. the door had vanished.	
		b. he could just see the shapes of the rocky columns.	

EXERCISE 6: COMBINING THE PHRASES INTO SENTENCES AND INTO A PARAGRAPH

Using *and, but, because so* and *when* to develop sentence structure.
Complete the following sentence stems:

Jack stopped at the entrance **and**_____

It was icy cold **and**_____

Water trickled down the stalactites **and**_____

Jack spotted the tunnel in the corner **and**_____

36 *'Language in action': coordination/subordination*

He spun around **and**_____

Jack waved his hands in front of him **and**_____

Jack stopped and listened, **but**_____

He hadn't gone far, **but**_____

He stumbled over a rock **and**_____

There were pools of ice at the base of the stalactites, **so**_____

He had only taken a few steps, **when**_____

Jack could only see simmering shadows **when**_____

It was a treacherous, winding path between the rocky columns, **so**_____

It was pitch black in the cave **because**_____

Examples

Jack stopped at the entrance **and** took in his surroundings.

It was icy cold **and** turned his breath into misty clouds.

Water trickled down the stalactites **and** collected in smooth, shiny pools of ice.

Jack spotted the tunnel in the corner **and** walked towards it.

He spun around **and** his insides twisted with terror.

Jack waved his hands in front of him **and** slid his feet across the floor.

Jack stopped and listened, **but** all he could hear was the drip, drip, drip of the water.

He hadn't gone far, **but** he had already scratched his knuckles and bumped his head.

He stumbled over a rock **and** crashed to the floor.

There were pools of ice at the base of the stalactites, **so** he knew he would have to move carefully.

He had only taken a few steps **when** the light vanished.

Jack could only see simmering shadows **when** he looked across the cave.

It was a treacherous, winding path between the rocky columns, **so** he prayed there was no trap he had not spotted.

It was pitch black in the cave **because** the door had vanished.

THE DRAGON

Clause (1)	Conjunction	Clause (2)	√
It was silent	**and**	a. he was sure the dragon was nearby.	
		b. all he could hear was his heart pounding in his chest.	
Jack's legs trembled	**and**	a. it took a huge effort not to run.	
		b. he did not run.	

184

A whoosh of air struck Jack in the chest	**and**	a. pinned him against the wall.	
		b. the dragon was coming nearer.	
Sweat dripped down into his eyes	**but**	a. he was terrified.	
		b. Jack dared not move.	
Its head was bigger than a boulder	**and**	a. he gritted his teeth.	
		b. it had scales like sharpened spikes.	
He still did not move	**but**	a. kept looking into its green eyes.	
		b. Merlin had warned him not to look away.	
The dragon's head slumped onto its chest	**and**	a. it was still awake.	
		b. its massive jaw dropped open.	
The enormous forked tongue hung out	**and**	a. it dribbled giant strands of slime from the corner of its mouth.	
		b. flicked from side to side.	
Its eyes rolled in its head	**and**	a. it crashed to the floor.	
		b. it could still see him.	
He was terrified it would wake up	**so**	a. closed his eyes.	
		b. he kept glancing up at the dragon.	
He eased the dragon's jaw open wider	**so**	a. he could see the fang.	
		b. it kept slamming shut.	
Jack had to push his hand through huge strands of dragon drool	**so**	a. it covered his hand.	
		b. his hand became slimy and slippery.	
The dragon bent closer	**until**	a. its nostrils were nearly touching Jack's face.	
		b. it could have a good look at the mark on Jack's hand.	
He kept glancing up at the dragon	**because**	a. he was terrified it would wake up.	
		b. its chest was rising and falling gently.	
He could see that the dragon was asleep	**because**	a. he was terrified it would wake up.	
		b. its chest was gently rising and falling.	

He had to grit his teeth	**because**	a. his stomach was heaving.	
		b. he had to hold his breath.	
It was hard to hold onto the fang	**because**	a. it kept slipping out of his hand.	
		b. it was covered in slime and slobber.	
He was rising to leave	**when**	a. he realized that it had gone very quiet.	
		b. he knew he didn't have long.	

EXERCISE 7: COMBINING THE PHRASES INTO SENTENCES AND INTO A PARAGRAPH

Using *and, but, so, because, when* and *until* to develop sentence structure.
Complete the following sentence stems:

It was silent **and**_____

Jack's legs trembled **and**_____

A whoosh of air struck Jack in the chest **and**_____

Sweat dripped down into his eyes, **but**_____

Its head was bigger than a boulder **and**_____

He still did not move, **but**_____

The dragon's head slumped onto its chest **and**_____

The enormous forked tongue hung out **and**_____

Its eyes rolled in its head **and**_____

He was terrified it would wake up**, so**_____

He eased the dragon's jaw open wider **so**_____

Jack had to push his hand through huge strands of dragon drool, **so**_____

The dragon bent closer **until**_____

He kept glancing up at the dragon **because**_____

He could see that the dragon was asleep **because**_____

He had to grit his teeth **because**_____

It was hard to hold onto the fang **because**_____

He was rising to leave **when**_____

Examples

It was silent **and** all he could hear was his heart pounding in his chest.

Jack's legs trembled **and** it took a huge effort not to run.

A whoosh of air struck Jack in the chest **and** pinned him against the wall.

Sweat dripped down into his eyes, **but** Jack dared not move.

Its head was bigger than a boulder **and** it had scales like sharpened spikes.

He still did not move, **but** kept looking into its green eyes.

The dragon's head slumped onto its chest **and** its massive jaw dropped open.

The enormous forked tongue hung out **and** it dribbled giant strands of drool from the corner of its mouth.

Its eyes rolled in its head **and** it crashed to the floor.

He was terrified it would wake up, **so** he kept glancing up at the dragon.

He eased the dragon's jaw open wider **so** he could see the fang.

Jack had to push his hand through huge strands of dragon drool, **so** his hand became slimy and slippery.

The dragon bent closer **until** its nostrils were nearly touching Jack's face.

He kept glancing up at the dragon **because** he was terrified it would wake up.

He could see that the dragon was asleep **because** its chest was gently rising and falling.

He had to grit his teeth **because** his stomach was heaving.

It was hard to hold onto the fang **because** it was covered in slime and slobber.

He was rising to leave **when** he realised it had gone very quiet.

THE ESCAPE

Clause (1)	Conjunction	Clause (2)	√
The walls shook	**and**	a. the tunnel echoed with the dragon's piercing screech.	
		b. the dragon was thudding towards him.	
Jack pressed his palms to his ears	**so**	a. he could block out the high-pitched shrieks.	
		b. he could still hear the shrieks.	
The stone throbbed	**and**	a. it was reminding Jack it could help him.	
		b. Jack slid his hand around it.	
The column of flames was heading straight for Jack	**but**	a. tore down the tunnel.	
		b. arched away from him at the last moment.	
The flames struck the wall opposite Jack	**and**	a. arched away from him.	
		b. tore down the tunnel.	

Jack didn't see the flames coming	**but**	a. he could feel their scorching heat on his back.	
		b. he was running down the tunnel.	
Jack saw a narrow beam of light ahead of him	**so**	a. the door was open.	
		b. he sprinted towards it.	
He dodged the rocky columns	**and**	a. ducked under the giant stalactites.	
		b. he didn't scratch his knuckles again.	
The stalactites collapsed	**and**	a. rained down from the ceiling.	
		b. crashed to the floor.	
Jack staggered backwards	**and**	a. stumbled over a rock.	
		b. froze.	
He fell onto his arm	**and**	a. he bumped his head.	
		b. a terrible pain shot through his body.	
Rocks crashed onto the floor all around Jack	**but**	a. he couldn't move.	
		b. he dived to the side.	
He was nearly at the end of the tunnel	**when**	a. he felt the ground start to shake.	
		b. he started running faster.	
He was halfway across the cave	**when**	a. a spear of swirling fire exploded into the cave.	
		b. he crashed to the ground.	
Jack's leg buckled under him	**because**	a. a stabbing pain shot through his knee.	
		b. he crashed to the floor.	
He couldn't see which way to go	**because**	a. he stopped for a moment.	
		b. he was blinded by dazzling sunlight.	
The door had disappeared	**when**	a. he looked round.	
		b. all he could hear was the dragon's roar.	

EXERCISE 8: COMBINING THE PHRASES INTO SENTENCES AND INTO A PARAGRAPH

Using *and, but, so, because* and *when* to develop sentence structure.
Complete the following sentence stems:

The walls shook **and**_____

Jack pressed his palms to his ears **so**_____

The stone throbbed **and**_____

The column of flames was heading straight for Jack, **but**_____

The walls struck the wall opposite Jack **and**_____

He didn't see the flames coming, **but**_____

Jack saw a narrow beam of light, **so**_____

He dodged the rocky columns **and**_____

The stalactites collapsed **and**_____

Jack staggered backwards **and**_____

He fell onto his arm **and**_____

Rocks crashed onto the floor all around Jack, **but**_____

He was nearly at the end of the tunnel **when**_____

He was halfway across the cave **when**_____

Jack's leg buckled under him **because**_____

He couldn't see which way to go **because**_____

The door had disappeared **when**_____

Examples:

The walls shook **and** the tunnel echoed with the dragon's piercing screech.

Jack pressed his palms to his ears **so** he could block out the high-pitched shrieks.

The stone throbbed **and** Jack slid his hand around it.

The column of flames was heading straight for Jack **but** arched away from him at the last moment.

The flames struck the wall opposite Jack **and** tore down the tunnel.

He didn't see the flames coming, **but** he could feel their scorching heat on his back.

Jack saw a narrow beam of light, **so** he sprinted towards it.

He dodged the rocky columns **and** ducked under the giant stalactites.

The stalactites collapsed **and** crashed to the floor.

Jack staggered backwards **and** stumbled over a rock.

He fell onto his arm **and** a terrible pain shot through his body.

Rocks crashed onto the floor all around Jack, **but** he couldn't move.

He was nearly at the end of the tunnel **when** he felt the ground start to shake.

He was halfway across the cave **when** a spear of swirling fire exploded into the cave.

Jack's leg buckled under him **because** a stabbing pain shot through his knee.

He couldn't see which way to go **because** he was blinded by the dazzling sunlight.

The door had disappeared **when** he looked round.

Part 4

'Language in action' templates

1. Plot outline
2. Scene outline
3. Collecting descriptive words and phrases
4. Sentence parts and structure
5. Stretching a sentence
6. Experimenting with vocabulary and sentences

Plot outline

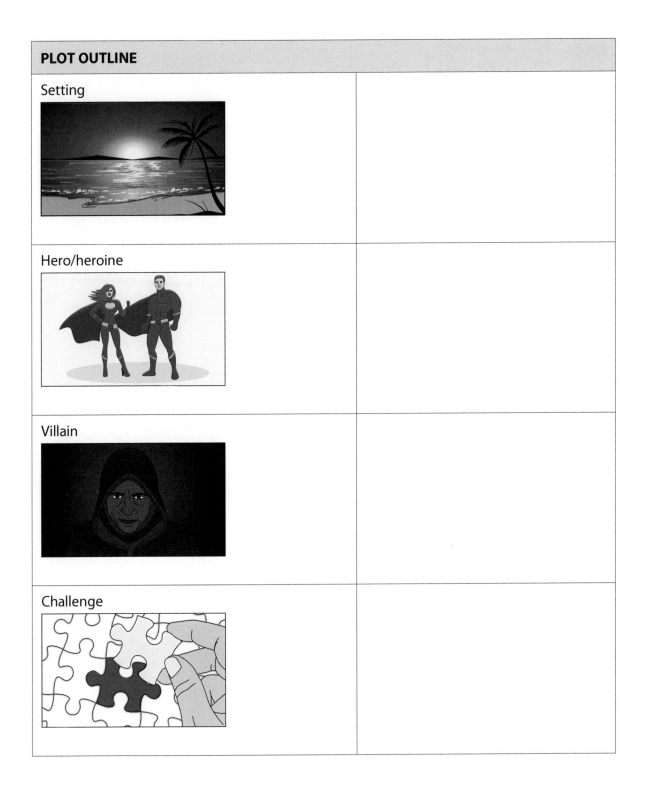

PLOT OUTLINE	
Setting	
Hero/heroine	
Villain	
Challenge	

Problem	
Result	

Scene outline

NOUNS

DESCRIPTION

DON'T FORGET
YOUR SCENE
AND
KEYWORDS

_____

_____

_____

_____

_____

_____

Collecting descriptive words and phrases

WORDS		PHRASES
NOUNS	**ADJECTIVES**	

Sentence parts and structure

Noun	
Verb	
Adjective	
Prepositional Phrase	
Sentence	

CHANGE THE NOUN

Noun	
Verb	
Adjective	
Prepositional Phrase	
Sentence	

CHANGE THE ADJECTIVE(S)

Noun	
Verb	
Adjective	
Prepositional Phrase	
Sentence	

CHANGE THE VERB

Noun:	
Verb:	
Adjective:	
Prepositional Phrase:	
Sentence:	

CHANGE THE PREPOSITIONAL PHRASE

Noun	
Verb	
Adjective	
Prepositional Phrase	
Sentence	

Stretching a sentence

STRETCHING A SENTENCE	
Who?	
Is doing What?	
When?	
Where?	
Why?	

STRETCHING A SENTENCE	
Who?	
Is doing What?	
When?	
Where?	
Why?	

Experimenting with vocabulary and sentences

STATEMENTS					

QUESTIONS					

EXCLAMATIONS

COMMANDS

EXPANDED NOUN PHRASES

SIMILES					

ADVERBS					

PREPOSITIONS					

CONJUNCTIONS					

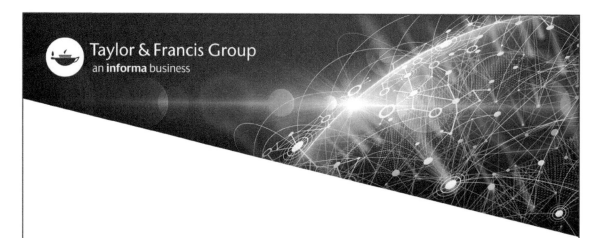